Celebrating Diversity

How to enjoy, respect and
benefit from Great Coloured Britain

ATUL K. SHAH

kevin
mayhew

First published in 2007 by
KEVIN MAYHEW LTD
Buxhall, Stowmarket, Suffolk, IP14 3BW
E-mail: info@kevinmayhew.com
www.kevinmayhew.com

9 8 7 6 5 4 3 2 1 0

ISBN 978 184417 823 0
Catalogue No. 1501037

Cover design by Sara-Jane Came
Cover image © Photographer: Varina and Jay Patel.
Agency: Dreamstime.com
Typeset by Richard Weaver

Printed and bound in Great Britain

'Dr Shah shares some very personal accounts of his experiences in this book to deliver his message fearlessly. His book contains practical examples of how each of us can become more respectful of difference.'
Vijay C. Thakrar – Partner, Ernst & Young LLP

'It is becoming ever more important to release the wasted talent and unrealised potential of so many of our citizens and *Celebrating Diversity* provides plentiful insights and a rich range of challenge to the status quo that should provoke valuable debate about how both individuals and organisations can find their own routes to embracing the benefits of our society's diversity.'
Keith Faulkner CBE, FRSA – Managing Director, Working Links (Employment) Ltd

'This book is a timely, articulate and thought-provoking contribution to this highly topical debate. Atul Shah makes a clear, enlightening and powerful case for embracing and celebrating diversity in all of its forms.'
Mike Waldron – Faith Regeneration Foundation

'This is a book based on experience which offers many practical examples of how we can all benefit if we cease to function "skin-deep" and positively embrace diversity.'
Cynthia Capey – Director, Suffolk Inter-faith Resource

'This is a must read for anyone that has a desire to be open-minded. It's a great check-list to ensure we are all-inclusive and forward-thinking in our ways. Written in the first person, Dr Shah makes this subject insightful and engaging.'
Raoul Shah – CEO, Exposure

'Practical, illuminating and very helpful.'
Lord Herman Ouseley – Managing Director, Different Realities Partnership Ltd

'An ideal corporate gift for employees, customers and suppliers – I have already ordered 25 copies.'
Satish Kanabar – Barclays

The whole world of diversity management and 'the celebration of diversity' in particular tends to lack any philosophical, creative, humanitarian and firm material underpinning . . . Atul K. Shah, on the other hand, in *Celebrating Diversity*, introduces a completely new dimension to what has become a legal as well as a social imperative in global society. His answer to his own question of 'how to enjoy, respect and benefit from Great Coloured Britain' is firmly anchored in a philosophical tradition and creative humanitarianism which is both practical and challenging. Appreciating no real disconnections between the spiritual and the secular, if humanity is defined in terms of sameness (essentially indivisibility and equality), diversity then becomes the norm: actually not only is it necessary for the survival of all aspects of society but, even more importantly, the understanding and practising of it represents a precondition for the acceptance of ourselves as individuals (identity) and, as conscious and socially responsible individuals, ourselves as moral and spiritual forces for change, improvement and the making of differences that matter.

Inspired by such philosophical humanitarianism and based on the experience of both being an East African Indian and a practising Jain in 'Coloured Britain', Atul K. Shah has written an insightful, creative and practically-orientated book which should be read, digested and acted upon by all who wish to make a difference and create a new kind of Britain – one in which all of us from different backgrounds will be able to share in and profit from, in all senses, a common future.

Professor Chris Mullard CBE

'Positive and Practical – A must-read book for all who seek peace and harmony and value difference.'

Lynne Sedgmore CBE, Centre for Excellence in Leadership

Contents

Foreword

What a pleasure this book is to read; it reminds us of the importance and advantages of celebrating and sharing diversity within the multicultural and multifaith society of Britain in the twenty-first century. Unfortunately, all too often we take this diversity for granted.

It is very illuminating to find someone who can share his personal life journey of living diversity on a daily basis in such an honest and authentic manner while threading through the text a sophisticated, thoughtful, integral and a complex analysis of the key issues of our time: including family and community relationships, equalities legislation, politics, the media, organisational life and religious belief.

The personal experience of being a 'minority' person – of having to 'fit in' is mixed beautifully with a wide range of informative views, facts and figures, useful resource information and pertinent quotes from a wide range of sources. We are left in no doubt of the importance of embracing and celebrating diversity and the advantages it can offer to every part of society, and to our own lives.

How many of us are brave enough to take up Atul's invitation to put ourselves in a situation where we are prepared to experience being in a minority, to really acquire the insight and empathy needed to improve and inform our own understanding and authentic living of diversity?

This book provides a fascinating and sensitive perspective on major issues within our society from a Jain pluralistic perspective and mindset. This is a perspective heard less frequently than many others within Britain today and Atul's book is a key contribution to introducing Jainism to the Western mainstream.

I recommend this book highly to you; it is thoughtful and at times challenging, provocative even, but always sensitive, intelligent and informative.

Lynne Sedgmore CBE
Chief Executive, Centre for Excellence in Leadership
www.centreforexcellence.org.uk

Dedication

I dedicate this book to all the champions of diversity who promote it with passion and persistence. I would also like to dedicate it to my parents, Keshavji Rupshi Shah and Savita Keshavji Shah, my brother Ritesh and sisters Dipti and Chandri and my wife Nina, daughter Jaina and son Meerav, and family members Indravadan, Jitesh and Sonal. Rakhee, Rajul, Payal, Miraj and Nihal, our nieces and nephews – you are our shining stars. Thanks for sticking by and being there through the rough and the smooth. I hope this book will help all our common futures.

About the author

Dr Atul K. Shah is an educator, scholar, journalist, speaker and broadcaster who has lived in Britain for 25 years. He has a PhD from the London School of Economics. As a social entrepreneur, he founded and edited the unique cultural magazine, Jain Spirit. He is an adviser to the BBC, and a Fellow of the Royal Society of Arts. Atul is founder and Chief Executive of Diverse Ethics Ltd (www.diverseethics.com), a company dedicated to providing diverse training, research and consulting to the private and public sectors; he is also editor of the monthly Diverse Ethics Bulletin. He is widely regarded as an outstanding speaker and journalist.

Introduction

Not a single day passes without racism or discrimination being in the news. Terrorism and suicide bombing have brought it to the fore, but these issues have been pervasive and influencing British society for a long time. Even as early as the 1950s and 60s, rental houses had signs saying 'No Dogs, Blacks or Irish'. There have been violence and even murders committed as a result of race. Equal rights for disabled people and gays are also very hotly debated. All this is surprising, given how Britain is a largely tolerant and accommodating nation, with a free press which is intellectually against racism.

Migration is a natural phenomenon – have you seen birds get a visa before they fly? Do elephants need a passport to cross the Serengeti Plain which is part of both Kenya and Tanzania? Have you seen trees distinguishing between their ethnicity and country of origin? What is not natural and obstructive is the drawing of borders and boundaries. This is the cause of so many problems today – and often we do not just draw physical borders – we draw mental ones too. And today this bordered world is conflicting with the borderless world of the internet and global transport and business.

And just as there has been so much media attention, there have been a lot of commentators. Frustratingly for me, a lot of the commentary has either been academic with people writing as if racism were a subject to be studied and pondered or by journalists who are themselves white with bordered minds and insensitive to the real issues. There is a real need for drawing from the rich experience of people who survive and prosper in spite of everything, and build bridges of friendship and cooperation. Often, these are the very people who never make the news because they do not seek publicity.

I was born and raised in Kenya by parents of Indian origin. I was a minority in Africa, and came to Britain at the age of 18 to become a minority here. However, there was a difference between the two experiences. Whereas in Kenya, I was allowed to be myself, here I had to somehow 'fit in', especially when I started working professionally. In writing this book, I draw on 25 years of experience of 'fitting in', something which the Indians have a reputation for being very good at. I have never experienced violence, although I did experience discrimination which was damaging, and at times felt much worse than physical violence as the scar would not heal.

In countries like Canada and even the USA, the racial integration and respect for diversity is very high and the achievements have been significant. One reason for this is that everyone is an immigrant so no one feels that the country belongs to them and they were there first. I worked for a year in the USA as a visiting professor and it was a remarkable experience – in fact, I found that a young Indian professor is considered to be a genius unless they prove otherwise. I felt privileged!

I write this book in the first person as I feel that is one way the issues can become real and the sensitivity to other cultures can be understood. I want to share my imperfections honestly, and also I want to share my desire and efforts to build bridges and connect with one another equally honestly.

I have spent a lot of my time working for charities and community organisations, which has given me a special understanding of grassroots issues. Unfortunately, we live today in a world of experts who specialise and study, but often cannot connect. The professionalism also often gets used to profit rather than to help or cure. I am not claiming that I am an expert, but I am saying that I have tried to live with diversity and have experienced its strengths. I have learnt a lot from British society that I never knew. For example, politeness, punctuality, appreciation and diplomacy are critical skills for success in any career. Good organisation, administration and law and order also help create and sustain a better society. Studying to become a professional and then working as one also taught me about professionalism and its importance in the modern world. The English language has now almost become my vernacular, and is for me a passport to the whole world.

My experiences of assimilation and settlement have created an identity crisis for me. I have changed career four times, and I am only 45 years old. At times I have struggled to fit in. Often I have excelled, but that excellence became a threat to others. This book is drawn from this rich field of experience. I have lived and worked in three continents and come from a culture of a fourth. This experience is going to become much more commonplace in this world of globalisation. Most migrants do want to get on with their lives without causing harm or injury to others. I also do believe most immigrants are grateful to Britain for allowing them to make a new home here and to build a new life. Fortunately, many indigenous British people are grateful to the immigrants and welcoming of the diversity which is such a strong fabric of Britain today.

My culture and upbringing have also given me a unique borderless way of thinking and assimilation which has helped me to live and make a home in Britain. I find this lacking in modern Britain, partly as a result of our history and our educational systems. It is said that experts are people who know more and more about less and less. My definition of community starts from the family, extends into the neighbourhood, the town, country and planet, and universe, each one merging into the other without boundaries. I have an inbuilt instinct and enthusiasm to help and share what I have with others, see and learn from the best in others. In addition, I have a sense of duty to my parents and past generations to leave behind a sustainable legacy and a light footprint. I draw from my own culture and religion (Jainism) in many parts of this book. Religion for me is not a dogma but a sustainable way of living. This is the real meaning of the word 'dharma'. I hope therefore that the reader will not interpret this as a religious book, but as one informed by different ancient cultures and philosophies, especially those which have stood the test of time.

My white friends say that this is where there is a major difference in the mindset. For them, things have to be organised, clear and structured so people know their place in the hierarchy. In contrast, Indian culture does not operate in such a structured or regulated manner, and is therefore difficult to understand and respect. Even faith is expected to be ordered, with priests, defined ceremonies and hierarchy – whereas in India, there is no such order. This is a big difference and, as a result, first impressions, perceptions and expectations are also very different. While there is definite strength in order, there is also weakness as it can distort spontaneity and the human spirit.

I hope that the examples and suggestions given help readers to negotiate their own paths of assimilation and transformation. There is no one right way, but there are alternative paths and methods of negotiation and assimilation. Values are the key to practising and embracing diversity. This book is written as much for ethnic minorities as it is for indigenous 'white' people (who are also not the same). For me, living with diversity has been an enriching experience overall. As a small-town boy born in Mombasa, Kenya, I have travelled far to come back home – to my-'self'.

Many people have helped in the publication of this book: Cynthia Capey of EEFA very kindly introduced me to a 'local' publisher and helped break the biggest hurdle of getting my first book published. She also went through the draft manuscript in fine detail and gave me very positive and constructive suggestions. My publisher, Kevin Mayhew, took a personal interest in the book from day one – even though he had not met me. Delian Bower, my editor, encouraged me to write this book in my personal style. I am most grateful to my friends and readers, who went through an earlier draft with patience and perseverance, and helped make this a much richer book. They are Sally Harding, Walter and Dorothy Schwarz, Sonal Shah, Carol Mansell, Debbi Botham and Dinesh and Paras Shah. My family have become actively involved in the writing of this book, with young Meerav, who is 8, helping with the copying and filing and even ideas for the cover design! I dedicate this book to them.

Atul K. Shah

Spicy or Plain?

Masala is the Indian word for spice. Plain is the English word for bland or unsophisticated. How would we like our world, spicy or plain? If we are to go by food preferences, then 'foreign' food is very popular in Britain. Indian curry has been voted the most popular dish today. The answer is 'definitely spicy'! But what happens when we go away from food into our choice of friends and neighbours? Here it seems our tastes are very different. A survey by the Commission for Racial Equality showed that over 90 per cent of the 'white' British population could not name a single close friend from an ethnic minority. A similar result applied to ethnic minorities – they had very few white friends. There seems to be a 'ghetto' culture – we like to live and hang out with familiar people. We prefer plainness.

Plain is familiar, spicy is risky. Plain is comfortable, spicy takes us into the unknown. Even when we order curry, we want to eat it with a fork and knife at a time and method of our choice, with plenty of lager. In India, curry is eaten with fingers and there is no lager to wash it down. 90 per cent of the time, the curry is vegetarian and has no meat in it, whereas here, we only think of chicken tikka masala. It seems we are happy to experiment with food, but wary of experimenting with people. And generally speaking, food is eaten early in the evening and not late in the night in India, as it is not considered good for digestion to eat and then go to sleep. So even our diverse dietary habits lack understanding and sensitivity.

Attitude

What is most worrying is that we are becoming a throw-away society – not just of objects, but also of people, cultures and relationships too. My wise mother often says to me in Gujarati, 'In today's world, only those people who are useful are valued – everyone else is ignored or bypassed. Be careful and choose your friends, because many will forget you if you are of no use to them.' How true. Could it be that we like spicy food because it is tasty and delicious and cheaply available – but do not care about the people who cook it or when they fall sick or have problems and need help? Could it be that we like migrants to the extent that they are cheap and useful, but do not want any other baggage from them like their different beliefs and cultures? If so, then we must remember that even though we may be 'successful' today, we can become 'useless' tomorrow if we have an accident or a health problem. Indian takeaway can be thrown away, but Indian people and culture cannot. It is better to live with respect for all in the here and now.

The reality of the modern world, with the internet, media, travel and international trade, is that people are being forced to mix. Masala is becoming the norm more and more. The person who is 'successful' is one who is able to adapt, assimilate and integrate. People are reacting to this challenge in different ways. Some are scared of it and go increasingly inward, trying to preserve their identity. Others see it as an opportunity to learn and grow, and have an open mind. There are many in the middle, who are not sure about which way to turn and are generally also confused about life itself.

Facts and Figures

The facts speak for themselves. A statistics pocket handbook on Ethnic Minorities in the UK sponsored by Lloyds TSB (published in 2004) examined a range of surveys and found that:

- The ethnic minority population grew by 48 per cent between 1991 and 2001 from 3.1 million to 4.6 million;
- The ethnic minority population is comparatively young. 45 per cent of the ethnic minority population is under 25, compared to only a third of the white population.
- By 2011, only 20 per cent of the UK workforce will consist of white able-bodied men aged under 45. (The remainder will be women, ethnic minorities and disabled people.)
- Students of Chinese and Indian origin obtain the highest levels of educational success at GCSE as compared to any other ethnic or social group, including the white population.
- White graduates are three times more likely to be offered a position by a top British company.

Colour Blindness

The most difficult thing to change in life is habit. If adults have grown in ghettos and not cultivated a habit of openness and respect, it becomes difficult to change at a later stage in life. The risk seems greater, and there is less time or patience to change and adapt. There is a fear of the unknown and a retreat into the familiar. Some adults have been forced to adapt — as a result of overseas travel for business or even an overseas placement, and have enjoyed the experience so much that they do not wish to return. For most, however, there are fleeting experiences of alien culture, and in a few cases, deeper ones through close friends and neighbours, or even mixed marriages. Some adventurous adults have discovered other cultures through travel and learnt from direct experience about the big wide world. Others have gone to the same places, but stayed on the beach and ordered fish and chips. Even when we have eyes, we are often blind. And those who are blind have more sight than we can imagine.

Trevor Phillips, Head of Commission for Racial Equality has stated:

> Behaviour in white Britain has not changed a bit. Last year, 94 per cent of white Britons said that all or most of their friends are white. This year it is 95 per cent. Once again a majority – 55 per cent – could not name a single non-white friend, and this was true of white Britons of all ages, classes and regions.

> What the figures tell us about the behaviour of ethnic minority Britons is even bleaker. Last year, 31 per cent of ethnic minority Britons said that most or all of their friends were from ethnic minority backgrounds; we found that this trend was stronger among the young than the old. This year the figures show a marked turn for the worse.

> The 47 per cent of ethnic minority Britons who last year said that most or all of their friends were white has now shrunk to 37 per cent; and the proportion who have mainly or exclusively ethnic minority friends has grown from 31 per cent to 37 per cent. This is way beyond any statistical fluctuation.

> It also remains true that younger Britons are more exclusive than older Britons. It must surely be the most worrying fact of all that younger Britons appear to be integrating less well than their parents.

> *Source: Isaiah Berlin Lecture, 2006 (CRE Website)*

What is Prejudice?

Prejudice is being redefined as time passes. It is not just about race or ethnicity, but also about gender, sexuality, disability and even ageism. There is a long human history of discrimination against women in many cultures in the world. It seems that, as a society, we are becoming increasingly less tolerant of difference. In spite of our better education and enlightenment, there is a growing sense of inequality experienced by many people. There is a direct connection between insecurity and a feeling of inequality. The more insecure people feel, the more likely they are to become prejudiced about something or other, and the more likely they are to feel prejudiced themselves. Could this be the product of an increasingly materialistic and faithless society? We will examine this in more detail in a later chapter.

The United Kingdom is becoming a melting pot of cultures, which started off as a legacy of the British Empire and the founding of the Commonwealth, but has now grown. I am a product of the colonies, born and raised in Kenya, and was a British subject from birth. I always had a right to emigrate to Britain and exercised this right after coming here to study in 1980. Participation in the European Community has also enhanced British diversity and, as English becomes more and more the international language of communication, more and more people come to study and work here. London is a growing world capital city. The United Kingdom is a society based on democracy, justice and liberty and has a history of tolerance and respect for other cultures. Also the geographical location and transport network make it possible for people from all over the world to travel here. People here are in general very polite, courteous, law abiding and respectful of one another. These are unique strengths and make me really proud to be British.

Diversity as Opportunity

This diversity gives us a huge opportunity to be at the forefront of global cultural change and makes us a key nexus for integration and global cooperation. It is a 'spicy' country, and how Britain deals with the spice will have ramifications for many parts of the world. So far, there is a positive attitude and government and the law are strongly pushing for diversity and equality in all areas.

The economic advantage of having ethnic minorities is significant and growing:

- Some of the highest educational achievers come from minority communities;
- They have over £25 billion of annual disposable income;
- They contribute more to the system than they take from it;
- They provide natural links to the global diaspora, opening global markets and outlets;

On the ground, there is some fundamentalism and resistance, but by and large, there is an acceptance of the idea of diversity and the reality of diversity. However, hitherto there is little pro-activity about diversity, and it is not seen as a priority and an opportunity for positive change and transformation by institutions, businesses or governments. Boards of companies are still fairly white and male dominated. The bosses may not mind recruiting from diverse backgrounds, but are reluctant to share power. The media is also very similar, except that the BBC have made radical changes (Zarin Patel is Head of Finance, Andrea Callender is Head of Diversity, Mary Fitzpatrick is Editorial Head for Diversity and Mihir Bose is Sports Editor). But generally speaking, power still rests with white people. There is a lingering 'institutional racism' which was identified in the Stephen Lawrence enquiry in 1999, and many institutions are resistant to change.

I am a Jain by culture, a word which few can spell. Even fewer have heard about Jainism, one of the oldest living religions of the world. I therefore belong to a minority group. As Indians are a minority, I am a minority within a minority. I have been living in this country for 25 years and have certainly encountered some prejudice. Visually, my complexion is black so I would stand out as different. Fortunately, affirming diversity is in my DNA, and as an Indian and a Jain, I have been brought up with an open mind and respect for other peoples, cultures and all living beings.

Biodiversity is not a separate issue

Jainism does not restrict diversity to humanity, but sees the entire ecosystem as diverse and all living beings as being worthy of equal respect. Human beings are just one of the species on the planet, and as we are on the top of the pyramid, we have a lot of power. But instead of using and abusing this power, Jains believe we have the greatest responsibility and accountability to other living beings. These are the values on which I was raised, and as a result, I feel they have given me a huge reservoir of strength in contributing to our understanding and practice of diversity in British society. My culture has taught me to seek wisdom wherever it may lie, and respect others despite their size, status or origins. Every living being is worthy of the highest respect. The sun never discriminates as to whom it shines its light on, so why should we? Jains take care not to harm even the smallest insects. We are all children of this vast planet, and there is room for us all. From a very young age, my family has taught me the highest level of integrity and humility. In fact, I have been taught to practise what I preach, so that my actions are synonymous with the things I write and say.

In truth, we are all different – no two people are exactly the same – we know this from our own families, let alone the outside world. It is a question of degree. Even we ourselves change over time and are different from one year to the next. Thus diversity is an individually experienced reality, not a choice or an 'issue'. How we choose to accept it and live with it is what this book is about. The most important barrier to valuing and accepting diversity is the mind, and this is also the most important resource for change and transformation. Later in this book, we will look at how we can cultivate and nourish open-mindedness.

Learning from Kids

Children are generally much more open-minded than adults. For very young children diversity is no big issue – they just want to play or paint or create with whoever is around them. Provided their actions and judgements are not influenced by adults or media, and they are exposed to different cultures, they can grow up quite broad-minded. I have made many friends from different backgrounds through my children. Their friendships encourage us to get to know one another. We recently had a dinner party at home with some 'English' friends and our son reminded us quite casually that if it weren't for him, we wouldn't have made these new friends!

Also at schools and colleges, young people are exposed to others from varied backgrounds and grow up having friends from different cultures. Universities in Britain are very mixed nowadays, so those young people who do go to university also get a fair exposure to diversity. We do not have data on how students mix when on campus. This is a time for building lasting friendships and breaking ghettos, as often the students live very close to one another in halls of residence. There are clubs and societies and international groups on campus which facilitate co-mingling. However, in my work at universities over two decades, I have seen that even here, many students stick to the friendly and familiar in the midst of significant diversity. The study of other languages, especially classical ones like Greek and Latin, used to be compulsory for many in the 1960s and 70s but then declined significantly. Nowadays there is an increasing emphasis given to the study of languages, although often the emphasis is on learning another European language, usually French or Spanish, rather than a broader choice which includes the nationalities and languages of other 'non-white' people living in Britain.

Work Conflicts

The real difficulties or tensions arise for adults in the workplace. Here, individuals have ambitions and aspirations and also personal values which may differ from the norm. How organisations accept diversity and deal with it can have important ramifications. Also how they deal with conflict is important – because conflicts do arise, locally, nationally and internationally depending on the size of the organisation or network. As a result of having an open workplace and a hierarchical management culture, it is often the case that conflict results in the individual with less power leaving the organisation. Rarely does it result in resolution or compromise. Hence the cause of the conflict can easily perpetuate. It is not surprising that when there was a public investigation into the murder of Stephen Lawrence in 1998/9, the team discovered that there was 'institutional racism' in the Metropolitan Police. This means that organisational structures in terms of recruitment, training and promotion are biased in favour of people from white male cultural backgrounds and against people from ethnic minorities. The enquiry was a major watershed in the British history of race relations.

Power and Control

In Britain, the statistics show that power in workplaces still rests among the majority white (mainly male) population. Hence conflicts, when they arise, are likely to be resolved in favour of the majority. There is a real pressure to assimilate and accept the values of the majority – at least in the workplace. To talk about faith or culture in the workplace is politically incorrect. This is only different for foreign-owned firms. In the public sector, again the mainstream culture and ethos is white. One of the things I discovered was that one should not question or challenge powerful people in these organisations – it is just not the done thing. If anything, one should suck up to powerful people, something which I found very difficult to do. In my culture, we respect elders and bosses, but there is no rule or norm which says that we cannot question them. In some British organisations, there is a thin veneer of politeness and openness, but underneath, they are run by bullies or a bullying clique who on the surface may be very polite. The traditional style of British management of organisations is hierarchical – few people at the top have significant power and a large number of people who actually perform the task of making the product or delivering the service generally have little power and influence in the organisation. Even when it comes to customers, those with the most power get the best service. Have you ever tried to make an insurance claim as a lone individual against a giant insurance company? They know you are powerless, and remind you of it.

Territorial-ism

Have you noticed how people on a train often take two seats instead of one because they do not want anyone to sit next to them? They do this instinctively without even thinking about it. If you want to sit next to them, you have to ask them to move their bag or paper so you can sit. This is a sign of a deeply held belief – many British people have a sense of territory and private space which they think belongs to them and is controlled by them. This is marked physically and mentally. This territorial thinking is a huge barrier to progress. If we reflect deeply, we are only temporary citizens on this planet and will not be able to take any territory with us when we die. In the case of public transport, which is publicly owned, we have no right over an extra seat, but we even seem to forget that. I found when working in public organisations that a lot of bosses had this sense of territory, even though the organisation was publicly owned and not their private company. I also know that this is practised by middle-managers and staff in private commercial companies as well.

For there to be progress, we need to do away with territorialism. We need to give space to others – physically and mentally. We need to understand that to possess and control is to become possessed ourselves. We actually lose power and control by acting territorially and become insecure. This is very hard to do in the modern-day materialistic society. However, it is something that we must learn and practise in day to day life if we truly believe in equality and diversity.

Identity Stress

What is even more worrying is the phenomenon of identity stress discovered by a recent Vodafone survey. Few employees identify with the values of the organisation they work for and they feel the need to change their values and identity to fit in and get stressed out doing so. Race is an important factor contributing to identity stress, although it is not the sole factor. The survey shows that identity crisis is not just an issue for immigrants but can also affect white people born and raised in Britain.

BRITISH BUSINESSES AT RISK FROM IDENTITY STRESS

Vodafone UK today warns that in a time when businesses are increasing their commitment to helping staff achieve a better balance between work and home life, the intended benefits are being undermined by 'identity stress'.

According to Vodafone UK's latest Working Nation report, a UK-wide study into identity in the workplace, workers are routinely changing their identity when they clock on. This tendency towards 'Jekyll & Hyde' behaviour is having a damaging impact on careers and social lives.

The survey of over 2500 workers, employers and entrepreneurs found that 58 per cent of people change their personality and identity to fit in at work.

More worryingly, there is a hardcore of 1.5 million employees (6 per cent) who feel compelled to change their identity completely. These 'identity-stressed' workers are three times more likely to work for companies that oppose their own values and twice as likely to lie to succeed and let colleagues take the blame for their mistakes. They are also twice as likely to be 'very dissatisfied' at work.

This conflict of values is not confined only to the identity stressed. Around 16 million (64 per cent) employees don't believe in what their company stands for and 15 million (58 per cent) change something about themselves to adapt.

As a consequence, a number of damaging behaviours are emerging in the workplace:

- 5 million (20 per cent) change their appearance significantly, 3.5 million (14 per cent) have modified their accent, 1.5 million (6 per cent) have concealed their religious identity, while 1 in 50 hide their true sexual orientation
- 29 per cent of workers are less true to themselves and less open at work
- Almost 1 in 3 workers (30 per cent) feel dissatisfied at work and almost 20 per cent are looking to move jobs
- 7 per cent of employees would lie and 11 per cent would be very ruthless in order to succeed at work, with men twice as likely than women to let colleagues take the blame for their mistakes, set up rivals for a fall or reject their own personal values to get ahead
- 1 in 10 employees say they are less honest in the work-place than outside it
- Almost 1 in 5 employers (18 per cent) have interviewed candidates who have assumed a false identity to help improve their suitability

These ill effects are carried over into the home – the identity-stressed are three times more likely to be 'very dissatisfied' in their life outside work and are more worried about the impact of work on their confidence, sleep quality, social life and self-esteem.

This negative behaviour not only affects morale – it can also impact productivity.

Source: Vodafone UK Workplace Survey, 17 July 2006

The above evidence shows that values can and do differ, not just between peoples and cultures, but also between people and organisations. Surprisingly also, these differences are not just due to race alone – for example, a white person may find it easy to fit in as a teacher in a school, but would not be able to work at all in a commercially aggressive advertising company. When politicians talk about shared British values, there seems to be a lot of disagreement about what exactly is common and shared in Britain today.

It appears that spice does give rise to conflict. Even in its nature, spicy food is hot and stimulates the body. For those who are not used to spicy food, it can lead to sweating! Similarly, those who are not used to sharing power and decision-making with people from diverse backgrounds can also sweat if they are not equipped to live with diversity. How do we deal with conflict? One way is to simply use power and quell the conflict by following the boss's command. I fear this is the norm. And it results in good people from different cultures leaving such organisations or becoming silenced and ignored or bypassed.

Law and Disorder

The law does protect employee rights and race discrimination is treated very seriously, so employers have to be very careful how they deal with such conflicts. However, many employees are afraid to exercise their legal rights, either because they are not aware of it, or because to exercise them is risky because they would be branded as 'troublemakers' and isolated within the organisation even if they win the case. Internal appeal systems are paper exercises. They simply do not work as they are controlled by the status quo. So to go to an employment tribunal to seek justice is lonely and isolating and used as a last resort when the individual is at the end of their tether and feels cornered and frustrated. Even if they find another job, the fact that a person took their previous employer to tribunal would act as a smear in the new job. Often, these matters are settled out of court, resulting in the ejection of the employee and the employer covering up their image and continuing the same behaviour.

Where there is a serious conflict in an organisation, this could be addressed by professional arbitration or getting an outside professional to bring the opposing parties together to discuss the conflict and the root source of it. If such a process is conducted with care and sensitivity, and with a clear commitment to a resolution for the purpose of the larger goal, then it can have a variety of outcomes – amicable departure of one or both of the parties, resolution and a stronger commitment to a shared purpose, or a forced resolution from the top which would leave a scar and a breakdown of trust among the conflicting parties. It is very likely that in reality, one party (usually the less powerful) leaves the organisation and there is little change to behaviour or internal structures or procedures.

Professor Cary Cooper has written in the foreword to the Vodafone survey:

> In my experience, the most successful companies stick to the following golden rules: ensure that senior managers walk the talk (actions speak so much louder than words); banish the blame culture and allow people to be more honest; manage people by praise and reward, not through fault-finding and negative feedback; celebrate and communicate individual and company successes; and finally, avoid unachievable performance targets or unrealistic goals.

The best long-term way to resolve conflict is through pro-active prevention. When an organisation develops a shared value system, and at the same time continuously celebrates diversity and creates open and non-discriminatory policies, it is less likely to have serious 'cultural' conflict. However, there are very few organisations today with such a mind-set or culture. There is pressure to change, and a few international organisations see this is an opportunity to strengthen and gain commercial advantage in a world which is becoming smaller and more inter-connected all the time.

Skilled Transformation

Even if we have the will, do we have the skill to make this transformation? Having a will creates a determination to adapt and change. Knowledge and information is now more easily accessible than ever before, and one of the best resources for transformation often already lie within companies themselves – their workforce. In places like Greater London, where 70 per cent of the entire UK ethnic minority population live, the workforce of most companies would nowadays be very diverse. If a school wished to teach Hinduism, it can look to its Asian staff for guidance in teaching materials, methods and festivals. A good facilitator who has worked with organisations or comes from a background of openness and respect for all cultures can be a very important help. Such a consultant can assist in charting out a strategy, deliver workshops and training, and facilitate better exchange within and a greater awareness of the existing resources within an organisation.

Suffolk Inter-faith Resource have invented a simple and effective Diversity Game which is having quite an impact nationally. Primarily based on faith, the game brings together people who work together and encourages them to understand different cultures and belief systems through interactive play. Players have to 'adopt' a faith for the duration of the game – they get a card which gives basic facts about beliefs. Challenge squares then provide opportunities for players to ask questions about these beliefs and to discuss a wide range of diversity issues. The results are quite astonishing – often people do not want to stop once they have started! And the players discover for themselves how much resource there already exists within the organisation and how much they can learn from one another. Thus it is possible with creative methods to bring about organisational transformation, where there is a will.

Media Power

The media has a major impact on our perceptions of one another. Television is one of the most powerful media, and the internet is also becoming very important, especially with the availability of broadband. How spicy is modern television? Well, certainly the colours are changing and the subjects are changing too. The BBC comedy *Goodness Gracious Me* and *The Kumars at No. 42* were both satires on Indian life in Britain and became huge successes, not just among Indians but across the country, attracting a varied and diverse audience. More generally too, television is certainly changing and we see more and more 'coloured' faces and an active attempt by TV companies to capture diverse audiences and cover wide-ranging issues. Some gay broadcasters are even given prime time media coverage – so sexuality does not appear to be a limiting issue. However, most visual media is limiting in that it cannot go into depth, which is often the strength of ancient cultures. It can open a window for interest, but this then has to be backed up by other media such as printed newspapers, radio, books and journals.

Music as Bridge-Builder

Music is also changing fast. Fusion music, which blends sounds and instruments from different cultures, and world music (original sounds from all over the world) are becoming infused into mainstream culture in significant ways. Punjabi MC is now being played in discos all around the country and bhangra music has become mainstream. This is having a big impact on young people – music is their language of communication. Spice Girls was the name of a famous girl band in the 90s – and there was one non-white member in the group. Music also crosses linguistic boundaries and can play a significant role in building bridges. The MOBO awards, which celebrate Music of Black Origin, have now become an international event. Live Aid was a concert which reached the whole world through television and was heard and supported by millions. My daughter has participated in a 'signing concert' (accessible to deaf people) and it had a huge impact and was broadcast on BBC TV. She was so touched that she now takes extra classes to learn sign language! It was the music which started her interest and respect for deaf people. In a similar way, drama and the visual arts can also play a very positive role in building bridges and showing the potential of a diverse Britain.

Rainbow Britain

As a country, we have the greatest resource on the planet – a very significant diverse population. It is difficult for us to realise, but very few countries in the world today can boast this diversity and geographical concentration – often, we take it for granted. The world is literally at our doorstep, giving us a huge opportunity for growth and renewal. No longer do we need the sun and the rain at the same time to create a rainbow – we have a rainbow 24/7. Travelling on an underground train in London, I would hear at least a few different languages being spoken in one journey alone. And often, I would not be able to tell which language it is.

The Mayor of London celebrates major cultural festivals at Trafalgar Square and this is a huge statement of diversity – people from different cultures and beliefs are an integral part of London and are welcome here. Diwali is now increasingly celebrated in schools across the nation in one form or another, not just by Hindu students but by all students. So is Eid. And this is a wonderful development – just as Christmas is celebrated by all, regardless of faith, so it is important that we are aware of different festivals and can share in them.

In my home town of Colchester, we organise the Navratri festival every year. It is a nine-day Hindu dance festival with live music, dancing, worship and sharing of 'prashad' (food). When we invite non-Hindus to participate, they find it difficult to believe that three generations are dancing together in circles in total harmony. There is no alcohol, yet everyone is having fun. Most of all, they get really touched by the warmth and hospitality accorded by everyone. They find it surprising that so many Indians live in the area – most minorities are invisible unless they appear together in a group. Hindu weddings are also very large affairs, with guests in the hundreds, with a thousand not being uncommon.

In-Sensitivity

To build bridges, the majority need to understand the minority and vice versa. To be a minority is to feel lonely and isolated. One way for the majority to understand this is to attend an event where they are a minority – and experience how they feel. For minorities, this can be an everyday experience. And they may even get used to it, but that still does not mean that they are being accepted. Just one warm welcoming and guiding hand can make a huge difference to the whole experience. This is how we can welcome minorities – by being sensitive to their needs. Often, immigrants are hugely resourceful and capable and want to live peacefully and amicably with their neighbours. The UK evidence shows that they make a huge positive contribution to the economy.

People from minorities also need to be sensitive about the majority. If they have been brought up in ghettoes or in isolation from different groups of people, then they will be nervous about 'different' people, not necessarily because they are prejudiced, but because they are unfamiliar. It will take time for them to understand and accept others, and we need to be patient. Ignorance does not equal prejudice, though it can lead to it. We need to be patient and pro-active in our efforts to share and inform, and there are some very easy ways of doing so which I have discovered from my personal experience. For example, white people love Indian food and especially home-cooked Indian food. We can invite friends, colleagues and neighbours to our homes and share a meal with them. This hospitality is second nature and can reap huge rewards in terms of relationship building.

As a family, we actively support the local school in their events, and my wife Nina goes around schools and community centres giving talks on sarees and playing dressing up with children. Old Age Pensioners in Clacton have become so fond of sarees, that they keep inviting her again and again! Through the Parent Teacher Association, we have organised three Diwali parties for parents and children which were a big hit. Each party was diverse – with kids rolling chappatis in one corner, men wearing sarees in another, and home-made Indian food served and Indian music played. It was educational both for children and parents in different ways, and a great ice-breaker given the modern media coverage about ethnics and terrorism.

Weddings and Feasts

In recent years, I have begun to notice a constant presence of non-Hindu guests at Hindu weddings. These are friends from school or college and colleagues at work of the bride and groom. For many of them, it is their first experience of a Hindu wedding – so eager are they that they are often the first to turn up on time! And Indian time is still respected in this country, so the Indians are the last, unfortunately. The priests are becoming familiar and are now translating the ceremonies into English to help the visitors, and surprisingly, in the process even Hindus are learning about their own culture and beliefs. When I attend weddings, I deliberately look out for the 'non-Indian minorities' and try and help them by explaining the ceremony or the food, even serving them a soft drink or generally asking them if they are all right. Often, I get asked lots of questions which shows the curiosity. Everyone is really drawn by the colours of the sarees and for many, the informality of the wedding is also a welcome surprise – they can bring their children without being embarrassed! Also I feel that 'white' culture is sometimes too territorial formal and soulless, and eastern cultures and even African culture has an informality about it which is very welcoming of 'outsiders' and feels non-threatening.

To sum up, 'spicy' is clearly desirable from any rational liberal perspective. What is required is a sensitivity to one another and a respect for one another, and an active dialogue and engagement on sensitive matters. Education is critical, not just in the form of books but also through direct experience. Patience toward one another also helps significantly, because it does take time to get to know one another. In our hearts and minds, we need to acknowledge the existence of other people and their rights to exist. White British people are generally private people and a little reserved – they value their privacy. Minorities need to be sensitive to that and find common ground on which to engage. Communication is key to building bridges, and the media needs to be sensitive to diversity. Communities are breaking apart as a result of modernity and this has an impact on harmony. Unfortunately, race and ethnicity can become a scapegoat at a time of individual stress. In the next chapter, we look at the role of God in creating or inhibiting diversity.

CHAPTER SUMMARY

- In terms of friends, Britons prefer familiarity to difference.
- Habits and mindsets are hard to break.
- Understanding others requires empathy and open-mindedness.
- Prejudice often stems from personal insecurity.
- The UK is fortunate to have such a cosmopolitan population.

- Organisations are generally reactive about diversity and rarely pro-active.
- Jain and Hindu culture integrates diversity with bio-diversity – there is no boundary – all living beings are worthy of respect.
- Children are a unique resource for learning about diversity.
- Work is often a place of cultural conflict, especially where an organisation is hierarchical and power rests with white people.
- Many people suffer from identity stress – their personal values differ from work values.
- Law protects the employee against discrimination and employers have to be very careful.
- Organisations should be pro-active about diversity and use creative methods to build teamwork and cohesion.
- Awareness and training about diversity should be on-going.
- The media have a major influence on our perceptions of others.
- Music and the Arts are beginning to embrace diversity through fusion.
- Bridges can be built through sharing and understand-ing at community events.

POINTS TO PONDER

- Migration is a natural phenomenon. Borders are not. We need to think and act 'outside the box'.
- Are you spicy or plain? Spicy food comes from spicy people – you can't have the food without the people.

- Where do you learn about other cultures and how do you learn?
- When you travel do you meet and engage with the local culture or stay on the beach?
- How do you choose your friends? Are they similar or different culturally?
- Are you sensitive to the needs of others?
- Do you feel insecure?
- How many languages do you speak?
- If you have children, do you observe and make new friends through them?
- Is your workplace/organisation reactive or pro-active about diversity?
- What is your taste for music and arts, and do you explore new sounds and images? How creative are you?
- Are you conscious of the different ways in which the media can influence your perceptions of others?
- Do you attend local cultural or community events and if so, do you engage and welcome different people?
- If we want to be respected, we have to learn to respect others also.
- Communication and dialogue are key bridges of diversity and should be kept open.
- Diversity begins at home.
- Misfits don't have to be chucked out – we can always make an alteration in our minds and hearts.
- Disability is in the mind.

God's Jargon

'If only God did not exist! Life would be so much simpler and everyone would be so much more respectful of one another.' This is certainly a commonly held view. However, like it or not, God is still very much alive in many people's minds. And we simply cannot ignore God. It is also true that few gods ever actively propagated violence, discrimination or racism because they were all for respect and love towards one another. 'So why is there such a mess?' you may ask.

One thing is certain: genuine atheists or humanists should not be against diversity as they respect all peoples and their rights to exist in this world. The logic and theory is simple, unless you believe in purity of certain races over others as Hitler did. This would make science racist, which also seems contradictory, at least on the surface, though there have been attempts by scientists to prove that certain races have a higher IQ than others.

Assimilation

When Zoroastrians (one of the oldest religions in the world) were thrown out of Persia and came to the shores of Gujarat in India around the eleventh century, the welcoming king asked them, 'How will you settle down and assimilate?' The leader replied: 'Please bring me a glass of milk and some sugar.' When this arrived, he put the sugar in the milk and explained: 'Can you see the sugar? We will be like the sugar. We will become invisible and if any-thing, sweeten Gujarat and India for you.' This has been demonstrated in fact – they are one of India's smallest communities but have a huge influence on the economy, which is totally out of proportion to their numbers. One of the largest Indian-owned multinationals in the world, TATA, was founded by a Zoroastrian family. It is a fasci-nating true story of peaceful co-existence based on faith. The secret to assimilation is to become like the sugar.

But God sometimes messes up equality and unity. Many feel that their religion is the only true religion or is superior to other religions. In this way, difference becomes noticed and sensitised. People begin to start to draw boundaries, make sweeping judgements, and become 'fundamentalist' about their faith. In the history of religion, many wars and battles have been fought over this, and there is a lot of blood on the hands of many religions. We must also remember that wars have been fought without the influence of religion, and humans have a tendency to fight for power or territory. It is, therefore, not fair to say that religion is the cause of all wars or without religion there would be no war. There are also different philosophies and world-views which have been called religion and have emerged from different parts of the world.

Forced Encounters

However, as travel and migration have increased, cultures and religions are forced to 'encounter' one another. This is when world-views come to the surface and become the subject of tension, or at the very least, debate and discussion. The global media also interconnects cultures and belief systems, enabling dialogue, or prejudicing the world against religion altogether. Modern British media is largely seen as anti-religion and anti-God. Just look at any newspaper and see how much space it gives to religions on an average day. And yet religion cannot be ignored as it is so powerful and influential. In Britain for example, faith is marginal to the coverage in the BBC – less than 5 per cent of all television coverage is related to faith. Even then, atheists complain that religion gets too much media coverage.

In Britain, the approach to other religions seems to me to be 'Christianised'. People start from the presumption that other religions are formal, have a priestly hierarchy, believe that there is only one true God, and have Sunday worship and so on. I still get asked about my 'Christian' name for example! This is unfortunately not seen by white people as a particular and biased way of looking at religion. Not all religions say that there is only one true God; not all religions have a priestly hierarchy; not all religions expect you to attend regular worship. There is much variety of belief out there.

Common Values

For example, the Sikhs believe hospitality and the sharing of food is very important to their faith. At the Gurudwara in Southall in London, they have a 'Langar' which is open seven days a week which serves fresh hot vegetarian meals to all visitors at any time of the day, cooked, paid for and served by the community. Hospitality is natural to the Sikhs and they have a special respect for visitors and travellers. This is diversity in practice – there is no discrimination to any visitor, irrespective of their colour or creed and all are treated equally. Also, there is no lecture about how we should all respect one another – it is a silent practical action. I feel that the Sikhs are a very important faith community in the heritage of Britain and we can learn so much from them.

It is also true that most religions are complex cultures and philosophies which cannot be simplified in a way that the modern 'no-time' human beings would like to understand them. Most people's views of other faiths are partial and based on stereotypes, e.g. Hindus have arranged marriages; Christians believe in everything Jesus said; Muslims are fanatics, and so on. Faiths and cultures have taken hundreds and thousands of years to be created and to percolate and survive in different parts of the world and cannot be summarised into a few rules or codes without reference to the larger context and belief system. There is also often huge variety in the way faiths are interpreted and lived by people in different countries or by different sects within the same faith.

Mutuality and Sharing

If we closely look at Britain today, communities are fragmenting everywhere. People often meet in the shopping mall rather than in a church or community centre. There is usually little time to even look at one another in the rush to shop and acquire. However, faith groups are still playing a positive role because they are bringing people together and connecting them and providing mutual support – something which would not exist otherwise. This mutuality is saving society and the government a lot of money as it is indirectly providing social care and support through voluntary organisations. My friends who live in York often let their home for free to a Christian community group when they are away on holiday. This enables those who cannot afford to go on holiday to have a break. Such acts of charity and selflessness are rare and an example of how many faiths are making a hugely positive contribution to modern society. Of course, none of it ever makes the news as it is not sensational enough.

Modern education systems are also mostly anti-religion and pro-science. Hence faith and its education is marginalised right from the very beginning, and put on the defensive. In the United States of America, the teaching of religion in schools is banned completely. This is because in the constitution there is a separation of Church and State. Paradoxically, it is a very religions country, with over 90 per cent of the population saying that they have some religious belief. As a result, many children grow up without any sensible discussion or awareness of faith whatsoever. What they are never told is that they are instead subtly asked to put their faith in the mammon of science and materialism, whose fundamentals are not always open to question. The belief in the non-existence of God is also a belief in itself. But it is disguised as logic. I do believe there are people who are secular fundamentalists.

Emotion and Belief

So in some ways 'God' does mess up society and present a challenge to harmonious living. One of the key reasons is that the very nature of belief is emotive. It is personal and a source of pride and passion. As a result, if belief is not tempered with reason and logic, it can spill over into intolerance and even violence. Hindu and Jain traditions have always been 'pluralist', never arguing that theirs is the only absolute truth and all other religions are false, but recognising the multiplicity of different viewpoints and the relativity of truth. Hence they have developed respect for other religions and if anything, suffered as a result of this through forced conversion by others. Some brands of Christianity and Islam are openly fundamentalist, believing that theirs is the only true God and the only true path to enlightenment. The Roman Catholic Church is an example of this. All others are either ignorant or false. In today's age of globalisation and science, it seems very difficult to find logical support for these strong viewpoints.

Faith traditions are the products of myth, ritual, stories, literature, art, philosophy, moral values, and human expression and interpretation. They may appear unified or be referred to as being one, but are rarely so. For example, the dominant western religion, Christianity, is divided into many different churches, although Roman Catholicism is by far the strongest. Within each tradition, there may also be conflict and a lack of unity. The Irish conflict between Protestants and Roman Catholics is a classic example. Furthermore, the character of Christianity and the practices vary from country to country. Thus even within a common framework and tradition, there is a wide diversity of practice. A simple example is language. Most sermons are given in the common language of the people living in a particular country. In the case of Christianity this varies from Spanish to Portuguese, German, Italian, Kiswahili, English and so on. I know that in Kiswahili, Jesus is called Yesu. What may appear on the surface to be homogenous, is in reality far less so. And vice versa – what appears to be different, may in reality be the same.

In truth, there are no clear boundaries between religions. Does anyone know where Judaism stops and Christianity starts? What is the boundary between Islam and Christianity? Hinduism, Buddhism and Jainism in India have a wide range of overlapping beliefs. I would say I am Hindu and Jain at the same time. Hence boundaries are a human creation and more likely to be associated with modernity and imperialism. In their essence, faiths are borderless.

Tradition and Conservatism

Leaders of large churches and congregations are often conservative and hold on to the past or a certain interpretation of it as that is their way of supporting their leadership. It becomes an anchor and rod of authority and status. However, the world is changing under their very feet very fast. Also, it is very difficult to keep on translating the ancient message to relate to the fast-changing world. As a result, young people are largely missing in all religions as they find it irrelevant to their lives and to their futures. The greater the traditional hold in any religion, the further young people run away, unless the gurus are modernisers and creative in translating ancient wisdoms to appease the new generation. The evangelical churches such as the York Rock Church, are attracting younger people because they are much more positive, lively and jovial and less formal and traditional.

In my own Jain tradition, there is no creator God, but we recognise gods as divine beings. For us, our Tirthankaras (Ford Makers) were teachers and role models who showed us the path to self-realisation. They conquered their inner self and vices to attain perfect knowledge and wisdom. Each soul is potentially divine and capable of realising their own inner purity. Some describe Jainism as a non-theistic tradition because of the way we view God. It is very difficult to explain Jainism in the West as it is not a religion in the conventional sense.

Pluralism and Modernity

The Swaminarayan Hindu Mission: Bochasanwasi Akshar

Purshottam Sangh (BAPS) is an interesting example of change and transformation which has led to significant growth and progress worldwide in a short span of time. Originating from Gujarat in India, BAPS has now got temples and communities all over the world, with over 100 new centres in North America alone. Many of their saints used to be doctors, scientists and engineers who are now monks and busy translating the faith for the western audience in an authentic and accessible manner at the same time. They use multimedia, exhibitions, live performances and theatre and even have their own IMAX film which is shown at their new world centre in New Delhi. Here, BAPS teach Hindu values through the fun, entertaining and interactive method started by Walt Disney but now translated into the teaching of timeless wisdom. This is educational and entertaining spirituality, which is taking India by storm and helping it to revive and retain its ancient heritage through respect and understanding. In particular, children and young people are drawn to it – something which is rare in most religions today.

When I talk to ordinary people, one of the biggest concerns is that of proselytising and conversion. In Christianity and even in Islam, it is often seen as a necessity to share the word of God with others and some preachers ask their followers and congregations to go and convert others. This is most difficult to accept in the modern world of liberalism and freedom. I personally find it difficult to understand why such acts are not illegal. There have been a few times when people have knocked at the door or stopped me on the street to share the word of the Bible, and when I engage with them and tell them that I am a Jain, they insist that I should read about the true word of God and learn from the Bible. There is a persistence which is simultaneously deaf and noisy. Some of the Muslim terrorists that have been caught in the UK have been found to be recent converts who have been brainwashed in a short time. I also know that some of the rich American churches regularly send their missionaries to developing countries with the primary aim of conversion. Hindus and Jains by and large do not act in this way, and rarely force their beliefs on others. Proselytising does not respect diversity nor the human rights of others to independent mind and thought.

How do we genuinely create a God which respects diversity? Or should we even think of creating such a God – as it would inevitably divide and disturb? What are the key differences between an Abrahamic and an Indian conception of God? Can these be reconciled? Alternatively, isn't it far better to teach people about the science of diversity without reference to any God? These are critical questions. And there is no easy quick-fix solution. No matter how hard we try, we will not be able to stamp out God or religion. Neither could we create a God just for the sake of promoting diversity. Instead, we have to work through the process of education and use media, to show the diversity that already exists within faiths, and the way in which different faiths talk about respect for others. In Christianity, there is the commandment 'Love Thy Neighbour' and it does not say 'Love Thy Neighbour – only if he or she is Christian'! Also, we can remove ignorance through positive exposure of people to different cultures and faiths, to a positive demonstration of their strengths in a way which ordinary people can relate to.

No Copyright

In truth, God has no copyright, nor did he or she claim

copyright. It is often the interpreters or middlemen who try to claim it, for the sake of territory or power or ego. In the Jain tradition, truth is relative and depends on the perspective of the seer. There is no absolute truth or one right way – only relative truth/s. The Jain philosophy of Anekant acknowledges the presence of multiple perspectives and the non-absoluteness of truth. It is a much more complex philosophy than is described here, and a sophisticated analysis of the different dimensions of truth and understanding. In practice, Jains have a very long history of tolerance and respect of other faiths and belief systems. Even today, the leaders of some Hindu and charitable/social organisations in the UK such as Lions, Rotary and Sewa International, are Jain. In Leicester, there is a Jain who has become a Christian minister, yet he is not treated as an outcast.

Interfaith Harmony

India is a very good example (although not of course perfect) of religions and cultures living alongside one another for thousands of years. As far back as the second century BC, Emperor Ashoka pronounced that someone who criticises another religion or sect for the betterment of his own is actually harming his own sect and creed. In the sixteenth century, the great Moghul emperor Akbar was a model of tolerance and respect for different cultures and traditions and in his own court, some of the most senior advisers were non-Muslim. He organised many multi-faith gatherings inviting Hindus, Christians, Jews, Buddhists, Zoroastrians, Muslims and even atheists long before the convening of the first World Parliament of Religions in Chicago in 1897. The most famous speaker at this parliament, Swami Vivekananda from India, started his speech with

the immortal words: 'Brothers and Sisters of America . . .'
The General Commander of Akbar's armed forces was a
Hindu. There is no real boundary in India where one religion
or belief system ends and another begins. Christianity
came to India in the second century, long before its arrival
in England and it is still being practised there and tolerated.
The Jews have been in India for 2000 years and never been
persecuted. This concept of boundary is problematic,
because it creates separation and division, territories which
cultures or peoples can conquer and control. In reality,
truth and God have multiple facets and flow from one to
another and have no defined territories or colours or even
master races.

Men in the Middle

And what do we do with the 'middlemen'? Yes, they are
quite often men and in the middle. This is a difficult
problem – as often middlemen have a lot of power and
are insecure because of it. However, it is possible that in
time, many of these middlemen would have retired and
for church or religious organisations to attract and retain
new young blood, they would be forced to change and
innovate. At present, the traditionalist churches are all
struggling to attract congregations in the West (although
Indian Christians have been noted for being among the
most regular attendees). Fortunately also, there are some
middlemen who are sincerely trying to change and mod-
ernise and do not believe there is only one God or one
way to Truth and Wisdom. Sai Baba, Ama and the late
Father Bede Griffiths are examples of such saints.

Mixed-faith marriages were rare in the past but are not
uncommon today. If the couple are both non-practising,
the faith differences may not matter so much. However, if

they are then these differences can come to the surface, especially around issues such as which faith to bring up their children in. In some cases, e.g. where one partner is Muslim, the family insists that the other be converted to Islam otherwise they would not be allowed to marry. This is a cause of much tension and anxiety especially for the family who has given away their daughter to the marriage. They do not like being converted to a different faith from the one in which they were brought up. From a macro perspective, mixed-faith marriages can be seen as a positive force in bringing about respect and pluralism in a multi-cultural society through bridge-building. However, for the individuals themselves, it can be a difficult experience, and although we do not have actual data, it is possible that many of these end up in divorce due to profound cultural differences. Those which succeed survive usually because one of the parties in the marriage completely accepts the faith or lifestyle of the other.

Culture and Religion are often Intertwined

Culture and religion are deeply intertwined for many people, and they cannot easily be separated. The way they live is not different from what they believe. This is most visible in India, where images of Gods are prominently displayed in businesses and shops in which personal shrines are created. Even taxi drivers have an image prominently displayed in the car for the purpose of their morning 'puja' (worship). Where God is such an integral part of people's lives, it is important that, somehow, they are made aware that their God respects other gods and it is OK if he or she is not the only true God. A family of gods could equally be worshipped on special multi-faith days to promote tolerance and respect. What needs to be avoided is a message from the pulpit which says that ours is the only true God and all else are false or inadequate. In the Jain/Hindu tradition, we even have gods which are connected to specific family lineages and communities, and these are still worshipped to this day. In a practical way, these gods help us keep alive the family unity and awareness of the lineage. So while it may be possible to separate religion and state, we should try not to ask a person to separate their religion from him or herself.

Religious Education

Another way of building bridges is to try to understand different gods and religions. In schools in the United Kingdom, the National Curriculum is promoting multi-faith awareness through the religious education syllabus. Not only are all the children enjoying the different colours, stories and variety, but so are some parents who discover other religions through their children's reading or homework! In the school where my daughter goes, RE is compulsory at GCSE level and the school only teaches Christianity and Moral Philosophy at this level. All of a sudden, the multi-faith teaching that was being provided has now stopped, with the result that a lot of the children are upset, even those who are from Christian parentage! However, the school cannot provide a more diverse education.

I do believe that if we are to promote pluralism, then children should be given the choice to study different faiths at least up to GCSE level so that they are exposed to different world-views from their classroom. The beauty is that in Britain today, there are temples, mosques, gurudwaras, synagogues and churches all over the country, so the children can actually go and visit these places for themselves. In this way, they can complement their studies by seeing the faith in its living context and grow up to be much more respectful and tolerant of difference. We are very fortunate to have a whole mosaic of faiths available to us at our doorstep and can use live tours and contact as a way of learning and experiencing different belief systems.

I am an adviser to the School of Oriental and African Studies of the University of London and helped them establish their excellent Centre for Jaina Studies. Similarly, I am closely connected to the Victoria and Albert Museum. What I have discovered is that there is very little funding and resources available for the education of ancient cultures in the UK universities. For example, there is not a single lecturer of Jainism throughout the UK whose post has been funded by the Department of Education and Skills. Professor Richard Gombrich of Oxford University also told me the same thing – for decades he has tried to get the UK government to fund Buddhist Studies and has not managed to get a penny. This is most surprising at a time when the UK is promoting diversity – this policy needs to be corrected immediately and we should pro-actively spend resources in cultural education at all levels, including Higher Education and Research if we are to truly create a better Britain.

Disagree without being Disagreeable

Understanding different faiths and belief systems can take a lifetime and more. Not many of us have the time, patience or skills to do so. However, we do somehow have to live with one another in peace, and understanding does help to build a deeper respect. What needs to be appreci-ated is that when trying to understand another human being, the reference point should not be ourselves and our world-view, but the other person and their world-view. This is very difficult to apply in practice but at the very least needs to be understood. We can disagree, without being disagreeable.

Dialogue and understanding are keys to building bridges and respect. However, in the case of believers, dialogue can be an emotive affair where boundary lines are drawn and people do not wish to change their habits or world-views as a result of learning something new from another faith. I have attended or participated in many interfaith dialogues or seminars where faith leaders come together. Instead of genuine debate and discussion, what we get is a loaded debate or no debate at all. Each faith comes to talk about how important peace is to them and they all meet one another and depart with a 'superficial' respect. There is no genuine engagement and each is proud of their own faith and its greatness. At the most, the faith leaders agree not to criticise another faith publicly. At a more grassroots and informal level, there is dialogue and engagement, and people are much more open to sharing and discussing as they are not bound by any official views or standpoints.

The complexity of faith and its emotiveness creates problems for modern-day technocratic society. A friend of mine, who is a manager, once told me: 'It is so much easier to deal with machines than with people!' We simply do not have the time and patience to understand one another, let alone learn about different faiths or belief systems. We want everything instantaneously, and if there is a conflict, we want it to be resolved so that we can get on with the work in hand. We want a patch or quick fix rather than a lasting solution as there is simply no time. What this means is that fundamental disagreements get constantly swept under the carpet and when they do surface, they erupt like a volcano.

No Patience

This is one of the major causes of faith-based tension today. We simply do not have the patience to try to understand one another even though external forces have brought us together to live in one country or neighbourhood. If there is respect, it is often superficial rather than real. In the 'What's in it for me' society that we live in, we only respect those who help us directly and are beneficial to us. If our neighbour the Sikh invites us to his home for dinner once in a while, we will think that Sikhism is good, but would not reciprocate by inviting our other neighbour the Jew to our house for a meal, taking forward the hospitality we learnt from the Sikh. No, because it takes a long time and effort to cook a meal and what is the point in befriending the Jew if he always keeps to himself? We have not understood the nature of unconditional hospitality which is central to the Sikh tradition. I often hear people complain that white English people love to visit others but rarely invite others to their homes, especially for meals. Here, we have not learnt or are unwilling to change our habits.

We are also living at a time in the West where there are more non-believers than ever before. As a result, there is also conflict and mistrust between the believers and non-believers. Many non-believers think that religious people are superstitious and irrational and should be avoided in any serious discussion or debate as they do not have anything to add. The intelligent media primarily presents this view, and there is rarely any space for writers from faith traditions. By and large, the mainstream media in Britain is secular. This also means that it does not play a useful role in building bridges of understanding, respect and tolerance between faiths.

Science and Religion

The dominance of a western scientific and materialistic world-view in our educational system also has a significant impact on our attitude to faith and belief and the promotion of religious pluralism. If God has no space in science, history, geography, mathematics, English, technology, sports, then what is the scope for education to give an important place to belief and faith in human life? In the eastern traditions, God is not sidelined but seen as part and parcel of everyday education and upbringing. Yoga is a very popular method of physical fitness today, and is intricately linked to anatomy, physiology and psychology – mental, physical and emotional health. It is a holistic science which does not belong to any particular faith tradition (but is a part of many) and if taught in schools, would be very beneficial on several levels. However, the perception is that it is somehow 'religious' and cannot be taught in the curriculum. The European Enlightenment has a major influence on the educational curriculum today, but there was also an Indian Enlightenment which was far older than the European Enlightenment, yet is not even mentioned or taught in British schools. Black History Month is celebrated every year in this country as it is believed that the perspective of history as viewed by black people is very different from what is being taught in schools today. Their history is ignored, corrupted and bypassed and there is now an active attempt to raise awareness by the black community.

A multi-faith perspective on diversity could lead to a much richer understanding about life and society and could also help improve our educational curriculum. It should not start from a basis of fear of the unknown, but from a genuine desire to learn and respect. There may be some losses along the way, but there will also be far more gains at this transient time. The vision of creating and benefiting from a truly diverse society should also be kept clearly in focus along the journey. There will be clashes between traditionalists and modernisers, but provided these dialogues are undertaken, then progress will be made. There is no holy grail which we can latch on to, but we will have to work collectively to evolve a diverse society.

It is true that God does create tension for all of us in building a pluralistic society, unwittingly. However, we cannot do away with God, so we will have to find creative ways of carving a respectful dialogue. A good example of newly designed buildings which can influence such reconciliation is St Ethelburga's (www.stethelburgas.org). In the heart of London, St Ethelburga's also provides a new multi-faith space which is designed as a circular tent and facilitates dialogue and discussion between different faiths. A circle has no one central authority or right path and connects different people. It is a few minutes from Liverpool Street station and was built to replace one of the oldest churches in London which was destroyed completely by an IRA bomb in 1991. The concept of this beautifully designed serene space, with a garden outside is to connect, inspire and rejuvenate. I see no reason why such a 'tent' cannot be replicated throughout the country to encourage different cultures and faiths to come together and work out a peaceful dialogue and way forward. It could be an open public space for peace and mutual respect where people of any faith and none can go to meet, reflect and connect.

CHAPTER SUMMARY

- Religion sometimes creates divisions.
- Globalisation forces cultures to inter-mingle and cooperate.
- In UK, there is a Christian-centric view of all religions.
- Religions are complex and not always easy to simplify.
- Break-up of communities affects our respect for one another.
- Religious education needs to be plural and accessible to all.
- Belief is by nature emotive.
- Faith is borderless.
- Traditions resist change and adaptation and are by nature conservative.
- Prosletisation and conversion are wrong in this day and age.
- God has no copyright.
- Middlemen sometimes influence interpretation.
- Culture and religion are often intertwined and cannot be seen separately.
- We can disagree without being disagreeable.
- Patience and tolerance are connected.
- Believers and non-believers have too many walls between them in Britain today and this is wrong. They need to keep active dialogue.

POINTS TO PONDER

- Faith can be personal without being impersonal.

- Try to see others as humans first and believers second, and you will see that there are no explicit boundaries between faiths.

- Belief is emotive – when one engages with people from another faith, one should be careful about the emotion and try to explain in a simple and open manner.

- Believers should be careful that emotion does not over-rule rational solutions.

- There is a difference between original faiths and interpretations of them, and we need to be alert to inaccurate or manipulated interpretations.

- For many people, their way of life and their belief cannot be separated and we should understand and respect this.

- Religious Education provides a unique opportunity to teach students different cultures and beliefs.

- We should develop patience, especially when we encounter different kinds of people, and give them the benefit of the doubt.

It's Illegal!

Discrimination of any kind – race, gender, sexuality, disability, religion or age, is illegal. The law in the UK is evolving all the time, but its principles are clear: discrimination is abhorrent and people of all races, sexes, ages and beliefs should be respected and treated with dignity. Overall enforcement of this law will now be in the hands of the Commission for Equality and Human Rights (CEHR) which will have significant resources and powers. If such discrimination happens in the workplace, the disenchanted employee can take the employer to an employment tribunal, where the burden of proof is on the employer and the liability, if proven, can be potentially unlimited. Thus it is a very serious issue and concern, and employers all over the country are being trained to ensure that they act fairly. Bosses have to be very careful in what they say and how they say it, and their actions also have to be as unprejudiced as possible.

The basic philosophy behind the law on Equality and Human Rights can be summarised from this paragraph in the Equality Act 2006, whose mission is to encourage the development of a society in which:

People's ability to achieve their potential is not limited by prejudice and discrimination, there is respect for and protection of each individual's human rights, there is respect for the dignity and worth of each individual, each individual has an equal opportunity to participate in society, and there is mutual respect between groups based on under-standing and valuing of diversity and on shared respect for equality and human rights.

The law on employee rights is very rigorous in this country and protects the employee in many different ways. Where there is a discriminatory incident of any kind, it has to be dealt with very sensitively by the employer. Even if in the end the discrimination is not proven at a tribunal, the whole affair can be very messy, cumbersome and costly for the employer in terms of legal fees and time. For the employee, discrimination is clearly an unfair experience, and the law gives significant rights to obtain redress and compensation.

Employee Protection

Specifically, there are rules protecting employees against the following types of discrimination – gender, marital status, gender reassignment, pregnancy, sexual orientation, disability, race, religion or belief, age, part-time work or fixed contract work. This is an extensive and exhaustive list. For example, if you feel you are being passed for pro-motion because you are pregnant, that can count as unlawful discrimination. Similarly, even part-time workers have certain rights. Sexual orientation should not be a reason for dis-crimination in the workplace in any circumstances. Thus there is considerable protection for employees.

There are different types of discrimination which have been defined – direct and indirect. Indirect discrimination can arise where, for example, all employees are required to be clean shaven – this could discriminate against Muslim men and is illegal. Harassment and victimisation at work is treated very seriously. Any offensive or intimidating behaviour which aims to humiliate, undermine or injure its target is also illegal. Bullying in the workplace by bosses, or if an employee is treated less favourably because they have complained is also counted as harassment and victimisation.

Redress

However, the reality is that few employees know their rights about discrimination and how the burden of proof is often on the employer. The employer has to show that they have not been discriminatory – not the employee. The other issue involved in a complaint is that it is very lonely and scary. The only support one can get is from the Trade Union, but the quality of that support varies. Even if you win, you lose because you become marginalised and identified as a troublemaker. Therefore, the only sensible option, once an individual makes a case, is to leave the organisation. What are the consequences after you have left? Will another employer take on someone who has made a complaint or taken an employer to tribunal?

All these subtle pressures mean that it is not easy for an employee to demand fairness even if that right exists in law. There is clear protection in the law against such victimisation – it is illegal for firms to bully or threaten people who have complained about discrimination. Often, such cases are settled out of court and the employer agrees to give a positive reference to the employee as part of the settlement. This keeps the matter secret and does not jeopardise the opportunities of getting another job. It also ensures that the employee leaves, thereby freeing the employer.

Disability

For people with physical or other disabilities, jobs are very few and far between. I have been to very few organisations where there are disabled staff, and private companies are the worst in this respect as they rarely employ disabled people. The new laws on public access has meant that workplaces are now accessible, or should be. However, disabled staff are still not recruited because of prejudice. And it is very difficult for disabled people to prove prejudice at an application stage. An organisation can simply say that the other candidates were better qualified, and the applicant would have very little information to prove that this was not true. So they never enter the system. There is a way in which people can complain about discrimination at this stage, and there is legal protection for doing so. Public bodies are being forced to be more representative and fair, and are now consciously having to give some jobs to disabled people.

When anyone is denied the right to work, there is a denial by society of their right to have meaning and purpose in life and to have the dignity of self-fulfilment and self-worth. This is a very serious prejudice. However, in reality it is much more difficult for disabled people to be able to prove prejudice from organisations that refuse to give them work, usually by not even giving them an interview. Individuals generally do not have the power or resources to take organisations to court. By definition, employers tend to be larger, more resourceful and more powerful.

Discrimination in other arenas, for example between neighbours or volunteers in a small local organisation is not easy to resolve as, unlike in the workplace, there is no formal legal structure to protect the individual and they have to make a complaint and take the action to County Court. This can be a costly and cumbersome affair. Racial abuse of any kind is a criminal offence and there are special police helplines in every area where complaints can be made. Where there is physical harm, then it is a police matter and a serious offence.

Institutional Discrimination

In terms of racial discrimination, the Race Relations Act 2000, which was amended after the Stephen Lawrence enquiry, covers the added dimension of institutional discrimination. Stephen Lawrence was a young black teenager who was brutally murdered in an unprovoked racist attack in London in 1993. The subsequent enquiry revealed that the police investigation of the incident was very poor and the police were found to be 'institutionally racist'. The organisational culture and structures were found to be racist and discriminatory and needed to be reformed.

The new law covers not only the behaviour of individuals, but also the structures of organisations. In particular, public bodies need to ensure that not only do they have fair practices in terms of recruitment and promotion, but also that the services they provide cater for the differing needs of minority communities. This applies as much to the police, as to schools, hospitals, councils, arts organisations, charities, libraries, GP and dental surgeries, and so on. It is a significant shift in the law, and places a major obligation on such organisations to change and provide services which cater for all, irrespective of race. If they ignore this requirement and are sued, then they can face serious consequences and fines.

One response to all this legislation has been of fear. People are increasingly attending courses on diversity training or being forced by their employer to do so as to ensure that no illegal acts are committed. As explained earlier in this book, the philosophy of diversity is one of respect and dignity for all, and therefore not difficult to understand. If conduct and character were based on this, then there would be no real problems because people would realise what a great opportunity diversity is for humanity. The legal pressure means that people are being forced to be much more conscious of their actions and this can lead to paranoia rather than a pro-active embracement of diversity.

Equality of Opportunity for All

In my experience, this is particularly true where organisational cultures have been white or predominantly white controlled and dominated, and are now being forced to change. The law is requiring them to be transparent, to report on their equality policies and practices, to have internal structures in place to monitor these, and adequate training and recruitment practices. Above all, they now have to be much more conscious about their actions, careful in their statements, and monitor their recruitment and employment practices. Some organisations react by becoming insular, following the paper-trail and documenting policies, without actually changing the culture and mindset. Other institutions embrace this change more positively and pro-actively seek out consultancy and guidance to make it. It is important to recognise that prospects for promotion depends on the opportunities and training and support given to employees. Denial of these opportunities to certain members of staff because of their ethnicity, gender or faith is also illegal.

One of my clients is a theatre company which is publicly funded and a charity. The Chief Executive Ms Dee Evans was honest when she said, 'We really need help as we do not know how to reach out to diverse communities and audiences, nor do we know what they would like to see.' I invited her to a community event, which she attended by taking time out from her busy schedule. In fact not only did she attend, but she also joined in the Navratri Festival and enjoyed the dancing. Then, in her speech, Ms Evans invited the whole community to come and see one of their shows, and promised to send complimentary tickets. Everyone was really touched by this, and she did follow it up and send a personal letter of invitation. The Indian community now have a close friend in the theatre and feel welcome there.

This is a simple and practical example of how small but important changes can be made to embrace diversity. Very often, people of all walks of life want to be respected and heard. Even if you cannot deliver everything overnight, the fact that you try to engage and listen is an important first step. Where an organisation engages in practical actions, such as the theatre above, even if not all communities or cultures are embraced, the fact remains that positive steps are being taken. This can help provide mitigating circumstances if any legal issues are raised in the future.

Change on the Way

From my research and investigation, it is clear that there are a lot of public organisations who will need to change and evolve in significant ways. They cannot simply hide behind their policy statements and say that we have non-discriminatory policies. For example, if the entire executive board and trustees of an organisation are white or mono-cultural, then warning bells should ring. This is where the power often rests, and it gives the impression that diversity has not yet been embraced at the top, suggesting that even lower down the organisation, the same is true. Also actions of organisations are visible and by looking at the website, the services, talking to staff, and observing the atmosphere in the workplace, you can get a sense of how 'diverse' it really is.

In education, there is still a lot of work to be done, especially where schools operate in 'ghetto' areas or where staff come from similar mono-cultural backgrounds and lack adequate training and support in diversity. The Department for Education and Skills is currently emphasising the slogan: 'Every Child Matters'. However, on the ground, it is far from clear how this practice has percolated. When we asked my daughter's secondary school to teach her Hinduism for her GCSE compulsory course in Religious Education, the school came back saying that they did not have the teachers to support her, although they were happy to allow her to study the subject: she would have to do it on her own. I wrote a letter and sought a meeting with the school, and had no response for three months. You would have thought that one of the first responses by educational authorities to the Race Relations Act would be to improve cultural awareness and training in schools. It is now seven years on, and the changes have yet to trickle through on the ground. As far as I know, there is not a single international/diversity multicultural event organised by this particular school in any year, and it has nearly 2000 students.

Increased Resources

What the law has done and continues to do is to prompt people to be much more alert about their actions than they were before. It has also led to an increase in resources and funding from central government and authorities to enable public bodies to make the transformation. I recently met some councillors who were very disappointed about some of the changes, asking me why there should be preferences given to minorities. For example, why is there such a thing as a Black Police Association? I politely explained that where there has been discrimination and prejudice over a long period, cultural change can only come about through pump-priming the system. For example, why would a talented and ambitious ethnic-minority person apply for a job in a predominantly white organisation if there was no protection or positive encouragement? In North America, they have affirmative action policies and race quotas for jobs and opportunities in all public organisations. This is done to redress the balance ensuring that there is a cultural and institutional change. Yes, this would cause dissatisfaction among some people who feel adversely affected, but it is hoped that over time, a natural balance would be struck and there would be genuine equality all round.

Perceptions and Barriers

Financial investment is also necessary to fulfil legal obligations. In terms of recruitment, job advertisements would need to be placed in ethnic media to reach targeted communities and ensure that minorities are aware of the opportunities that exist. It may surprise you, but for a long time I thought that the only work you can do for the police is to be on the beat or driving around in cars. There are a large number of people who work within the police but in the back office, doing research, administration, investigation, forensics, and so on, whom we rarely encounter in public. This misperception came about because we normally create judgements based on our experience. Now, there is an active campaign by the Police to go into communities and explain the various jobs that exist and opportunities for them. All this costs, in terms of time, skills and effort. Sometimes, it takes a coloured face to recruit another coloured face. So we need more ethnic minorities on the recruitment side also. My perception is that the whole human resources and personnel recruitment industry has serious diversity issues itself and needs to change. If the recruitment professionals are mainly white, then this would automatically create a bias in the whole system.

Public Services for All

The really huge challenge is in providing services to cater for the needs of minorities to follow the legal duty to make public services accessible to all. Suffolk County Council have produced a wonderful document – 'Aspiring to Inclusion' – which sets out the positive and practical steps local authorities and public organisations can take to be inclusive and give equality of access to all. It is a road map for diversity based on creative thinking and a genuine aspiration to change and evolve. Professor Tony Booth writes in his introduction: 'Inclusion is not about achieving perfection but about being willing to reflect, challenge and change.'

Let's go back to the theatre example I mentioned earlier. How does a theatre company cater to a diverse audience? Can it do so by producing diverse plays? Yes it can. Also encouraging diverse writers? Yes. What about the language the play is in and the scriptlines? What about methods of presentation? Clearly multicultural plays are better than 'pure' cultural plays in attracting large audiences, but it may still be necessary to do some 'authentic' cultural plays to show the varieties of values that exist within different cultures. Plays by African writers or Indian writers, and acted by modern actors, are an interesting way of opening doors to new cultures, provided they are promoted and seen by diverse audiences.

In education, the curriculum also needs to adapt and change. I remember once talking to a university lecturer in art history and saying how little of Asian art is taught in mainstream universities, even though we all know that it is vast and exists. Her reply was that unfortunately, there aren't enough 'experts' in the area. Here experts and the notion of expertise is culturally defined and in my view, can easily be discriminatory. What she really meant was that the person would need to have a PhD from a famous university and publish articles in quality scientific journals whose editors are specialists in European art! Indirectly, the definition of expertise then becomes discriminatory and exclusive. This is an example of systemic institutional racism.

The European Enlightenment is given huge coverage in the media and in art history courses, yet the Indian Enlightenment predates it by at least 2000 years and is rarely mentioned anywhere. It is not enough in these circumstances to say that because there are no experts, the subject will not be taught. Universities are now legally obliged to create the expertise, nurture it and encourage it and supply a diverse educational curriculum. They have to change and invest in the change. Black history is another good example of how the coverage of history is distorted from the perspective of many ethnic minorities who see white history as littered with blood, duplicity and exploitation. Quite often there is hypocrisy and selectivity in the way research is carried out and history is interpreted. In Australia for example, the slaughter of the Aborigines and destruction of their 20,000-year-old culture has been very devastating for the whole world. However, very little of this is talked about in schools or universities and the subject of history and its content now needs to be re-examined under the Race Relations Act. The 'colour' of history needs to change so that its interpretation is not prejudiced.

Justice and Fairness

Law and regulation are designed to provide justice and protect citizens. They are the primary means of attaining equality, protection and fairness in a democratic society. Institutions like the Commission for Equality and Human Rights, the police, law courts and prisons combine to give effect to law and ensure that people and organisations abide by them. Huge resources and expertise are poured into these systems, and when laws are passed, such structures serve to implement and enforce them. As a result, there is tremendous interest in diversity today from all arenas such as educational bodies, media, health organisations, county councils, arts councils, and so on. Special jobs are being created to champion diversity with titles like Diversity Manager, Equalities Officer and Head of Diversity and often teams are created under these champions to help them fulfil these roles. For public bodies, equality standards are also becoming important, and they are monitored and audited, ensuring that organisations adopt and implement diversity strategies. This is all excellent news for the creation of a truly diverse and open society.

Creating such posts however, does not mean that an organisation has changed. The power and resources given to the diversity manager and the level of authority and respect will make a huge difference to what is being really achieved. Even the human resources and personnel development professions need to ensure that they have a diverse membership as very often, the heads of human resources and personnel are the gatekeepers of an organisation and need to be sensitive to applicants from different backgrounds and beliefs.

One argument that is given by public bodies is that we rarely get quality ethnic minority applicants. It is true that finding them is difficult as there are no national media channels to reach such a thinly spread out and diverse grouping. However, if organisations are serious about having a diverse workforce, they need to go out into the communities and develop new ways of reaching them through internships and other innovative methods.

Variable Commitment

I have also found that the power and the resources allocated to diversity officers vary from one organisation to another. In some cases, these are contract or part-time positions, where a woman is appointed for one year, given a huge workload with little resources and very little power or seniority. There is little 'respect' for the diversity manager, and hardly any time to go out into the community to see what is actually happening. I know this because I have invited them to our community events, and even given them opportunities to speak. Also, there is a question as to whether diversity is a human resources issue or a service-oriented issue or both. In many cases, the organisation is still working at a human resources level and has hardly begun to look at services.

For public bodies, additional funding has been allocated from central government to help bring about this transition and transformation. However, when I asked some local councils how much is the funding and has it actually been spent on diversity matters, I have usually drawn a blank – there seems to be little transparency and accountability in this area. I am sure this is not true of all local authorities, but really it should be untrue for all of them as they are legally obliged to be diverse.

Fortunately, there are some organisations where diversity has become a natural act. I recently bumped into an Indian site supervisor of a construction company in London who has 30 staff working for him. He explained that his employees came from all different countries and were able to work together in harmony. I thought to myself, this is a globalised business, and we are unlikely to ever hear about it in the press, but it is so far ahead of its time. And none of the recruitment has been as a result of the Race Relations Act: it has been natural and unprejudiced, possibly because the boss himself is from an ethnic minority and hence does not have any fear or prejudice against immigrants. It is also possible that diversity is much easier to attain in organisations which do not have a history and are not large and cumbersome than in those which do. In large organisations, change has to deal with organisational culture and people issues, and it depends on the people in the hierarchy and their commitment to change. Also, change processes are much slower in large organisations than in smaller organisations.

Finding Diverse Employees

In terms of recruitment, some organisations say that they cannot find the right calibre of ethnic minority people to apply for the jobs. There are two issues here: one of awareness and publicity through alternative channels, and the other of getting people with the right qualifications and experience, especially at senior levels. If there has been prejudice in the past, it is unlikely that good black and minority ethnic (BME) people would have risen up the ladder to be able to apply for senior jobs. They would not have had the right opportunities and challenges, and many may have left because of the frustration. Also, it is not easy to reach BME people because there are no large national channels for reaching them through the media. All too often, they have existed at the fringes of society and even their media has rarely attained a national voice. Extra effort therefore has to be put into reaching ethnic minority communities by all concerned. The bosses do need to get out and reach into the communities. Investment also needs to be made into recruitment and training at an early stage and removal of barriers to internal promotion. Space needs to be created for all to grow and flourish without prejudice.

The law is helping the process of transition to a truly multicultural and non-prejudicial society. Along the way, there will be some teething issues and tensions, but if the goal is truly understood by all, and if the strength of diversity is to be embraced, then the journey will not only be comfortable, but fun too. Britain is very fortunate to have citizens from all over the world living here, and this benefit does not exist for all countries. Very few countries in the world today can boast such a diverse population within a concentrated geographical area. Also the world is increasingly getting smaller, so to have such a diverse population in one country gives it an enormous economic strength.

CHAPTER SUMMARY

- Law is very clearly against discrimination of any kind – gender, religion, sexuality, disability, age and race. The Commission for Equality and Human Rights has been set up to enforce these laws.
- Employees are protected by the law and have rights to fair treatment at every level in the organisation, including at the point of entry.
- Employers have to be very careful in their treatment of employees and ensure they do not discriminate.
- Compensation claims against employers can be costly and time consuming.
- Victimisation of individuals who claim their rights is also illegal.
- Institutional racism is also illegal – organisations have to have a representative workforce and provide services to cater for all kinds of people.
- Employers need to advertise jobs in ethnic and diverse media outlets and actively reach out into diverse communities to understand their needs and aspirations.
- Diversity Training and Resources need to be provided to help organisations change and adapt to the new legislation.

POINTS TO PONDER

- It is better to be pro-active rather than reactive.
- The law can lead to fear, but it should be turned into an opportunity to benefit from diversity.
- There is protection for employees if they feel they have been discriminated against – they can go to an industrial tribunal.

- Legal costs for employees to bring an action are usually covered by home insurance policies.

- There are very good websites and resources to help people understand the law – see the Resources section at the back.

Minds Wide Open

When we throw a stone into a pond, it ripples and sends small waves all the way to the edge of the pond. In the same way, all actions and attitudes begin with the mind, and have ripple effects over a large area. A boss's attitudes to his or her colleagues will often become part of the culture of the organisation, and services and recruitment will follow these attitudes. This chapter looks at the concept of a diverse mind, and the qualities required to develop and nurture it. It is as easy as it is difficult. All depends on how committed we are personally to practise and promote diversity. Often, children start off with that openness and respect for all. How we nurture them and retain this innocence is the challenge for our parenting and education.

All Action Begins with Thought

Practising diversity starts with the mind. What do we think of others? How do we judge them? Do we trust and respect them? Do we have preconceptions about them or any stereotypical views? All this will affect our attitude. This will then have an impact on our actions toward others. And as adults, we are often consciously or subconsciously shaped by our experience, learning and environment. And this creates habits of mind which can be limiting and partial. And like all habits, they can be hard to change. And Mahatma Gandhi said very beautifully: 'Be the change you wish to see in others.'

A simple way to start understanding diversity is to think how we would like others to treat us. Most people would like to be respected, trusted and loved. However, very few people are able to see beyond themselves – to translate this view into their attitude to others. And so far, I have only mentioned human relationships. How do we perceive animals and nature? How do they perceive us? As a Jain, I know that my tradition starts with a respect for all life, and the human being has the highest sense of responsibility and accountability to the universe. We are endowed with a superior intelligence and consciousness which is a blessing and gives us this additional sense of moral responsibility.

Respecting Bio-diversity

Irrespective of our personal beliefs, it is a fact that this world is a mosaic. The variety of species of animals and plants, the sea, the sky, mountains and rivers and different countries, cultures and landscapes create a tremendous diversity all around us. The only thing that affects this mosaic is our attitudes and actions. Have you ever seen a plant discriminate? Do animals choose their friends depending on their colour or species? Are insects worthless because they are tiny and not as strong as humans? For me, this eco-conscious perspective has subtly had a big impact on my psychology and attitudes to others, though I will admit that I am by no means perfect. As a Jain, I have never distinguished between human diversity and 'bio'-diversity. However, I read very little about this in the media and usually diversity is seen as a human problem and limited to a human context. For me, this approach to the question is limiting in itself, and therefore, the solutions, if we find any, will also be limiting.

True diversity requires humility and awe, especially towards nature. And herein lies our first major obstacle – the ego. We are proud and often self-centred, and this attitude blocks us from becoming diverse. In our minds, the pre-occupation is with me, I, mine. Often our world is quite narrowly defined to our personal family and friends and there is little room for others. If we come from such a world, then diversity will be very difficult as we would have very little exposure to the outer world, of nature, races and cultures. Either we do not think it exists, or we do not give it any importance. Our lives would be marked by narrow boundaries. This is clearly not true of all peoples, but very common in a materialistic society whose goal is possession and ownership.

Upbringing

Our upbringing shapes our mental outlook. If we are brought up in a 'ghetto', then we do not have much direct encounter with other cultures or peoples. This can lead to indirect discrimination of that which is unfamiliar and of which we are ignorant. Our experience and learning as children at school also shapes our attitudes. If we are raised in a multicultural environment, and if we have regular visitors to our home from different cultures and go to their homes, our children will see this as a strength and opportunity. For example, we have 'white' English friends living in York whom we visit once every year, and who come to visit us. They are older than us and do not have any young children, but still our children love to visit them because they are made to feel very welcome. When they visit us, it helps to show them that our hospitality is for everyone, not just our immediate relatives. As a parent,

I see this as the best diversity education they are getting – subtle, practical and removing barriers.

Recognising the incredibly rich and complex nature of reality, Jains developed the notion of the 'Many-sidedness' (*anekant*) of existence. This enabled Jain thinkers to affirm both permanence and change. The primary elements of substances are permanent. But the forms or modes of these substances are continuously changing.

Relativity

Emphasising the limits of ordinary knowledge, Jains developed the theory that truth is relative to the perspective from which it is known. Furthermore, because reality is many sided and knowledge true only from a limited perspective, all knowledge claims are only tentative having the form, 'A may be B', rather than 'A is B'.

The limitations of knowledge are illustrated with a popular Jain story involving five blind men and an elephant. A king once brought five blind men into his courtyard where he had fastened a large elephant and asked them to tell him what it was. Each man touched the elephant, and on the basis of their perspective, told the king what he knew this thing to be. The first felt the trunk and declared that it was a huge snake. The second touched the tail and said it was a rope. The third felt the leg and called it a tree trunk. The fourth took hold of the ear and called it a fan, while the fifth felt the side of the elephant and declared it to be a wall. Because each insisted that his claim was correct and truly described the object in question, the five men were soon in the middle of a heated argument. They were unable to resolve the dispute because they failed to recognise that each of their claims was true only from a limited perspective.

Like the blind men, each person perceives things only from their own perspective. These perspectives are determined by many factors, including socio-cultural conditioning, particular place, time, light, hopes, fears and, of course, are subject to the limitation of our sensory receptors and reasoning power. A person seeking profit sees everything in terms of gains and losses; an insecure person sees threats everywhere and a person devoted to God sees everything as God's blessed creation.

When it is understood that knowledge is limited by the particular perspectives from which it is achieved, it becomes easy to see that knowledge claims are conditioned by the limitation of the perspective that it assumes and should always be expressed as only tentatively true. Just as the blind men should have been more guarded, saying for example, 'Standing here, feeling the object with my hands, it feels like a snake. It may be a snake,' so should everyone understand that their knowledge claims should be asserted only conditionally.

Alternative Truths

Analysing the logic of conditional assertion, the Jains came up with a sevenfold schema for making a truth claim about any particular object. For example, the following assertions are possible with respect to, say, the temperature of a glass of water:

1. It may be both warm and not warm, depending upon certain conditions.

2. Independent of all conditions, the water is indescribable (all knowledge rests on certain conditions).

3. Indescribable in itself, the water may be said to be warm subject to certain conditions (a combination of 1 and 4).

4. Indescribable in itself, the water may be said not to be warm, subject to certain conditions (a combination of 2 and 4).

5. Indescribable in itself, the water may be said to be warm and not warm depending upon certain conditions (a combination of 3 and 4).

The reason why the last three assertions all begin with the claim 'Indescribable in itself' is that every substance known and described possesses an infinite number of qualities – each of which also possesses an infinite number of modifications. Although ordinary knowledge reveals some of these qualities and modifications, it cannot reveal them all. The eminent philosopher Alfred North Whitehead wrote about this by saying, 'We often mistake the map for the territory – the map is not the territory. It is merely a representation.' Thus, all descriptions of reality are only partial. The substance itself, with its infinite qualities and modifications, can be fully known only when all the limitations to knowledge are overcome.

Partial Knowledge

The sevenfold scheme of conditional assertion forces us to recognise the partial and incomplete nature of ordinary human knowledge. This is a very important initial step in overcoming the passions, because desire, hatred, pride, anger and greed stem from partial one-sided understanding of things dogmatically presumed to be the whole truth. How many times have we embarrassingly realised the inappropriateness of our anger, jealousy, pride, or greed when we came to see the 'full picture'? Greed for money vanishes when it is understood that money can't buy health, friends or happiness. Excessive pride gives way to humility when we come to appreciate the wonderful qualities and accomplishments of others. Anger and hatred disappear when we realise that other objects, situations, or persons are no threat to us. To the extent that we appreciate that the knowledge from which the destructive passions arise is partial, we are encouraged to restrain ourselves until our understanding increases.

In Indian culture, visiting homes is a very common social practice and also sharing food is a part of this friendship and hospitality. We find that this is a great ice-breaker and relationship builder. This is why we have so much 'social capital', as in times of difficulty, we come together and help one another. It has been carefully culti-vated and nurtured over time. Looking forward, practising diversity would require us to actively mix with different people and involve our children in this mixing.

Schools also make a huge difference to the 'mindset' cultivated in our children. In the UK, there are many schools where 'white' people are a majority and also schools where 'white' people are a minority. There are some schools which are ethnically mixed and varied, but a lot fit into the above category. Often, the way schools are composed is a reflection of the neighbourhoods they serve. Private schools (sometimes known as independent or public schools) are getting a good ethnic mix in places like London where the immigrants are also economically prosperous. However, I have noticed in these schools that most of the teachers are 'white' and so many of them do not understand the diversity that exists in the school and rarely provide diverse services to meet the mix of students that they serve. Parents of these children also do not appear to be active in demanding change, as often these schools are competitive to get into, and they are just grateful that their son or daughter has a place in the school.

Diverse Teachers

Having a mixed group of teachers from diverse backgrounds could make a huge difference to a school and its influence on the children's mindset and outlook. But I suspect that there are very few schools in the country which could boast a diverse teaching population. This process of change and adaptation will take time to seep through, and the government is putting more effort to attracting a diverse range of students into the teaching profession.

What I have noticed through the story books of my children is that the names of characters are changing, and so are the colours on the faces of their literacy books. This is a very powerful progressive way of introducing diversity. To my 7-year-old son reading these books, it subtly makes him feel accepted. If by chance his name is the same as that of a character, it would make him very proud indeed! At the Prettygate Infants school where he went, the head-mistress was always very keen on diversity and this year, he had the opportunity to conduct a Diwali assembly in front of the whole school! A 7-year-old gave a presentation using PowerPoint entitled 'My Diwali' which was personal yet open and sharing. He wore his traditional dress when making the presentation, and all the children were intent on listening to him. At the end, he gave 'Prashad' (food) to everyone, which is a practical way in which we share our Diwali. In this way, he was able to share his festival with others and felt very proud that day of his identity, not in a way that it is better than others, but that it is OK to be Hindu and to be a part of a larger and diverse whole. Even a few months later, the children were remembering his assembly and went up directly to him saying how much they enjoyed it.

Sharing Light without Losing It

For my part, I thought of a different way of explaining Diwali by doing a live experiment. I brought two different coloured candles, one was pink and small and the other was green and larger. I explained that Diwali was a festival of light – where we share our light with others and learn that genuine sharing does not lead to loss – instead, it leads to more light and happiness. I had a box in my hands which I gave to my son, demonstrating that when we give objects to others, we lose them ourselves. Then I took the smaller pink candle, lit it and brought it nearer the wick of the bigger green candle. This immediately burst into light. In a practical way, I showed how a person can give light to another, without losing his/her own light. And that was the essence of Diwali: to shine our own lights, and share these with others. The role of parents and teachers is to help us shine brightly, and our personal role was to share this with others without losing any part of ourself. Far from losing something, sharing actually strengthens and connects us to one another.

Light is natural and knows no boundaries. It does not say it will shine only on certain people or will stop shining after a certain length. Light tries to remove the darkness of ignorance and illiteracy. When our minds are open, we allow ourselves to receive light from others, irrespective of their ethnicity, gender, age or sexuality. We see beings as sources of light and wisdom, from whom we have an opportunity to learn and grow. If we wish to, we can have that early innocence of a child even when we are adults, without prejudices or any colour blindness.

Travel

Travel is a very important way of nurturing an open mind. And what is even easier is that in the UK, we do not need to travel far to learn about different cultures and beliefs. We have world class museums and galleries which also have different exhibitions running throughout the year. And these are spread out throughout the country, not just in London. Temples, mosques, community centres are springing up all the time in different parts of the country, and often, they are open and welcoming to visitors. Even during festival time, it is possible to share in the festival. You merely have to ask someone who is a member or telephone them. I recently showed someone the picture of the Swaminarayan Hindu Temple and asked them where they thought the place was. The answer was India. When I told them it was in London, they grabbed the flyer and kept it!

World travel has also increased considerably, and here there is an opportunity to go beyond the beaches and the night clubs to the local places where people live, eat and worship. Often, these places would be very different from the hotels and the beaches and the hospitality would be very warm and courteous as, in many cultures, it is an honour to have a guest. This is when one can not only relax but at the same time learn and grow. Just as a true scientist is mesmerised not by what he knows, but by what he does not know, so too a genuine student of diversity would be mesmerised by travel and make attempts to see the 'real' people and places in the foreign country then the 'surreal' hotels and beaches which cater for the tourist and are commercially oriented.

Practical Techniques

I believe there are four practical ways in which we can practice open-mindedness on a daily basis. These are:

- To uplift our veil of ego-centrism and acknowledge our interdependence.
- To be conscious of our own stereotypical views and generalisations.
- To be open to friendship and dialogue and not be afraid of learning something new which may impact our own habits and values.
- To practise forgiveness and be open to accepting forgiveness from others.

Controlling Ego

It is simple but often forgotten in the rush of modern society to practise diversity. We need to acknowledge other people's right to live and breathe and have dreams and aspirations just like us. We have to start from the basic belief that they have just as much an equal right as us to be on this planet. We should learn to see our skin not as a border or a superior colour, but simply as a layer of physical protection. Our minds must allow others' existence and not be swamped by our egos which say that all of life is about me, me, me. Then we cannot even begin to be diverse, as we do not acknowledge the real existence and desires of others. Jains have a core belief, 'parasparopagraho jivanam': all living beings have a right to live and exist and are interdependent on one another. If it weren't for the road builder, how would we be able to drive out of our homes to work every day so effortlessly? The street-sweepers and cleaners help to keep our environments clean so we may stay healthy and safe. We may not see them reading the news or teaching our children, but they are still worthy of respect. How often do we stop and say hello to them? For this to happen, our ego needs to be contained by humility and broad-mindedness.

Awareness

Secondly, we need to be conscious of our own stereotypical views and generalisations. For example, one extreme view can be that: 'All blacks are thugs and criminals'. This means that if we are to meet a new black person on the street or in the workplace, we would have a very different attitude to them, perhaps even be scared, so that we would never give them any work. We in turn (including me, because my skin is black) may feel that we always have to be on the defensive and explain that we are not thugs but good people. Often, our stereotypical views are subconscious and we may not even be aware of them. They are shaped by our experiences, media and friends and relations. What such views do is limit our minds from genuine respect of other people and pre-judge their character and behaviour. If we accept that no two people are ever the same, then at the very least, when we meet strangers for the first time, irrespective of their colour, we should start from a position of respect and give them the benefit of any doubts.

Another good example of a prejudice we may not know about is our faith in medicine. When we are ill, we would normally go to a doctor and put our full trust in him or her, even though we may not understand the science of medicine. However, if someone suggests that we should see a complementary therapist instead, we would have lots of questions: what are their qualifications? What is the guarantee that the treatment will work on me? Are there any side-effects? In the case of doctors, we do not ask these questions and have trust in them because they are regulated by government. However, it is possible that they are not perfect also.

Stereotypes and generalisations cannot be eliminated overnight. However, to be conscious of them and to consciously engage with people with an open mind is helpful to practising and living with diversity. It also allows us to be surprised and to learn something we had never known before, from all kinds of people. It requires us to listen more than we talk, to hear and learn rather than lecture and become deaf to others.

Fearless Dialogue

The third practical solution of open-mindedness is to remain open to dialogue and overcome our personal fears, prejudices or insecurities. This is difficult, as it has the potential to take oneself to an unknown territory and to learn that something that we had accepted as a basic truth for a long time (e.g. eating meat is good and healthy) is now understood to be a bad habit which is not only bad for our own health, but bad for the animals and the environment. This may lead to a major change in behaviour, which as adults we may be scared to implement as we feel it is much harder and we would have to learn a whole new way of cuisine and change our shopping and eating patterns. This is scary for anyone, but if we do achieve it, it has the potential to take our own quality of life to a very different level and increase our own self-confidence and fearlessness. This is an example of translating a change in the mind to a change in lifestyle, habits and action to accommodate that change. It requires courage and determination. Mahatma Gandhi was a unique soul, but this was one of his key qualities. If he was convinced about a new idea or way of living as being better than an old one, he would do his best to implement it in his own life first before even talking about it to others. It seems in the modern world, we do not feel we have to 'walk our talk' and there are so many examples of people in responsible and powerful positions living such double lives. Hypocrisy is very common in modern society and a truly diverse and open-minded society should not be hypocritical.

Perhaps another more personal example may help here. Our 13-year-old daughter was asked by one of her friends whether she wanted to join her Sunday Christian church group and meet other teenagers once a fortnight for a social gathering. Her instant response was yes, but she came to us to ask for permission. We come from a different religion, but in the small town where we live, our numbers are too tiny for us to have a regular teenagers' group, so we said yes. It is now almost a year since she started, and she has enjoyed these social evenings and made new friends. We have not noticed any change of attitude by her to her own religion or identity – if anything, it has strengthened it. Paradoxically, she is the only 'non-white' person in that group, and gets a lot of attention and respect from them. They value her involvement and friendship.

To have such a mindset, we need to allow ourselves to be questioned, including exposing the very core of our beliefs. It requires a degree of self-esteem and self-belief. It is much easier to criticise others than to criticise oneself.

We are often proud and our beliefs have taken a long time to evolve and become accepted and shape our very existence. Usually, when we go into conversation, we carry shields and daggers with us, without knowing it. And this can prevent us from being genuinely diverse.

Forgiveness

The fourth practical solution of open-mindedness is that we need to be ready to offer forgiveness and accept forgiveness. This is very hard to do in the modern world of pride and egoism, because to seek forgiveness is to admit a mistake or failure. For those in positions of power and influence, this is like admitting defeat. But to err is human, to forgive, divine. We can make mistakes, we can stray from truth because we are only human and therefore not infallible. In the Jain tradition, we have a special forgiveness prayer which we are supposed to recite every night to cleanse our minds and seek forgiveness from those whom we may have hurt, knowingly or unknowingly. It goes like this:

> Khamemi save jive, save jiva khamantu mein, mitti me savva bhuvesu, veram majja na kenai (I forgive all beings, may all forgive me; I love all equally and have no enmity towards them).

In this prayer, we also give forgiveness to others, those who may have hurt us, knowingly or otherwise. This enables us to free our minds of any baggage, pro-actively and positively.

Open-mindedness is not just a rational endeavour – it cannot simply be achieved by explaining the logic of diversity. It needs to be cultivated. It can be achieved and nourished through meditation and visualisation, creating a state of mind which is calm and collected, at ease with itself and the wider world which surrounds it. Any sincere practitioner of meditation would experience the mind as being part of a much larger whole, where one is merely a spirit in a vast ocean of harmony and interdependence. Practical techniques of visualisation would help us to see that often our quibbles are petty and mindless, influenced by greed and selfishness, and forget the vast time cycle of life in which we operate. If we are going to die, what is the point of being selfish? As Ted Turner, the founder of CNN, the global news channel, once said: 'There is no fun in being rich in a dying world.' We are a part of the future direction of this world, and can influence it positively through our thinking and actions.

For a mind to be open, it also needs to be free from clutter. As a Jain, I know that material possessions are a big clutter, and a Jain monk is nomadic and owns nothing and does not even carry any money. The fewer our possessions, the more at ease we would be to purify the mind and spirit and understand the needs of others. The more we possess, the more we feel duty-bound to protect, and a lot of mental energy will be devoted to this. Simplicity is the key to open-mindedness. Instead of creating the larger insecurity of depending on our material wealth and possessions, we learn to trust our own spirit and develop an inner security in this spirit.

Diet

In the science of Ayurveda, it is clearly explained that diet has an influence on the state of mind. Tamasic foods, such as meat, alcohol, caffeine, onions, garlic, excite the body and make it irritable and sensuous – as if the mind and body are on a rollercoaster. On the other hand, rajasic foods such as fruits, vegetables, salads, have a much gentler impact on the body and mind and help to keep it calm and balanced. The food we eat affects our circulation system and hormonal balance, and some foods can also 'clutter' the mind. In Ayurveda, the time we eat is also important to our state of mind and well-being, and it is advised that we do not eat late in the night – ideally before sunset. It is not good to sleep straight after eating a heavy meal, and generally, our digestive system gets slower and inefficient at night time. The health of the body has an impact on our state of mind, and therefore our open-mindedness and respect for others.

In summary, our attitudes and mental outlook are critical to the way in which we will embrace diversity. If we are minorities, we would like and expect the 'majority' to respect us. Similarly, the 'majority' would do well to embrace open-mindedness as it would help them to grow and live with dignity. There are practical techniques of cultivating and nourishing open-mindedness which would benefit everyone. Changing attitudes is the most important step in embracing diversity. It is not always easy to change the attitudes of others, but we can certainly change our own.

CHAPTER SUMMARY

- Open-mindedness needs to be understood, cultivated and nourished.
- There is no line between human diversity and bio-diversity – we are part of a much larger whole.
- Ego obstructs the mind.

- Truth is relative and not absolute. It is multi-faceted and multi-dimensional.

- Travel can broaden the mind.

- Four Approaches to Cultivating Open-Mindedness – Controlling ego; Awareness; Fearless Dialogue; Forgiveness.

- Diet can influence our attitude to others.

POINTS TO PONDER

- You may think you are open-minded but are you really?

- Do you cultivate and nourish open-mindedness?

- How often to you enter into difficult or challenging dialogue, and how often do you avoid it?

- Are you afraid of being confronted about your deep-held beliefs? Are you willing to engage with others about theirs?

- How aware are you of your own ego? Does it inhibit your respect for others?

- How often do you forgive and how often do you ask for forgiveness? Are you afraid to apologise? How willing are you to accept the mistakes of others?

- How often do you travel and do you go beyond the beach? Do you travel to diverse places within Britain?

Working Together

Organisations have cultures. And cultures work in organisations. Where they blend together and cooperate and learn from one another, diversity becomes a strength. Where they do not blend, or where one culture dominates the hierarchy and mode of operation and demands others to follow suit, there is discord and a serious possibility that the law is being broken.

The composition of staff in an organisation depends on many things – where it is located, the kind of work it does and whether or not it trades globally. Similarly, the culture of the organisation depends on whether it is British-based or foreign-owned, and the commitment and character of the leadership to openness and diversity. For example, in the town where I live, school teachers, especially at primary level, tend to be white and female. This may be a result of various factors such as the nature of the work, the holidays suiting women who are working mums, the wages, the composition of the population in the town, and so on. If minorities are less than 5 per cent of the population, it may be difficult to get teachers from ethnic minority backgrounds to apply for jobs, let alone recruit them. In London, it may be impossible not to have teachers from ethnic minority backgrounds. Such is the composition of the population.

Hierarchy and Power

The traditional model of organisation in Britain is still

hierarchical, with power residing at the top of the pyramid. Hence organisational cultures are dictated by behaviour at the top and the attitude to diversity that is cultivated at that level. If the board of directors is diverse, that would send a bold and positive signal not only symbolically, but also through the actions and communications. A survey of the top 100 British companies showed that very few of them (less than 10 per cent) are diverse at the directors' level, as most executive directors are white and male. Similarly, just 18 per cent of MPs in the House of Commons are women. In the public sector, there is an even bleaker picture – despite the fact that 4 million women are in the public sector compared to 2.4 million men, women hold a minority of the senior posts. This survey by the Equal Opportunities Commission in 2004 notes:

> Most organisations go on having the same kinds of people in the driving seat, despite the fact that women's and men's roles are changing, that there are increasing numbers of older people and disabled people, and that there is a growing ethnic minority population. Public, political and business life in Britain is massively unrepresentative of British Society: it's not democratic, it's not balanced and it's not good for business.

The poor representation of women in senior positions in business is also not a good sign, especially as most large companies trade globally. There seems to be a ghetto culture at the top, and executives only want to share power with those whose culture and values are similar to their own. One of the most senior women at a major banking group, Claire Bright, sued the company for unfair dismissal (*Guardian*, 12 May 2006). She made a complaint about her male boss, whom she described as having an 'egotistical and mercurial character' and a 'boorish and undermining' management style. In summation, Bright maintained that her boss put her down because he 'could not manage a clever and successful woman'. So it seems smart women are a threat. As one eminent recruitment consultant, Helene Martin-Gee told me recently, 'There simply is very little imagination in British Boardrooms.' Diversity does require imagination and a keenness to adapt to change, even if it means cultural change.

Work as Meaning

For individuals, work is a significant feature of their lives. Happiness and contentment at work can make all the difference between success and failure in life itself. It is a means to earn a living and also a method of personal growth and progress. It provides purpose to people's lives, giving them dignity and self-esteem. Fulfilment at work has a ripple effect into the rest of their lives, and failure can have the opposite effect, leading to low morale, lack of confidence, stress and maybe even family breakdown. It is vitally important that, as a society, we create harmonious workplaces. The statistical evidence from a variety of surveys shows that this is unfortunately far from the truth.

When different cultures come to work together, there will be differences in the values and the methods of operation. I can give an example from my own experience. In mainstream British culture, if you ask someone of equal rank to do something for you at work, you are obligated to return that favour to them. Ideally, one should offer the trade-off at the time of the request. I never knew that. I come from a culture where give and take is natural and does not have to be reciprocated by the same people. I can give to one and take from another without expecting a return from the same person. It took me a while to realise that I need to be careful in my actions at work and I even found that at times when I gave selflessly, I attracted suspicion. What is his motive for doing this? Does he have a hidden agenda? This creates tension and if there is no communication, it festers and hurts. It has taken me decades to understand that to be too enthusiastic and from a 'foreign' culture is not a good thing in large British organisations.

Diverse Teams

How then do we work together if we come from different cultures? Group tasks and challenges can force us to cooperate and learn each other's ways of working. When a difficult goal is accomplished by a diverse team, it can help build bridges and enable individuals to see the strengths of different perspectives and how they can combine to achieve a larger outcome. Awareness training about different cultures and ways of working can also help significantly in shaping diverse workforces. Often when companies acquire foreign subsidiaries, the executives undergo cultural training so that they learn the different ways of working in foreign lands. The cultural difference between Britain and America may be smaller than say the difference between Britain and India or Britain and Japan. Increasingly, they try to use existing staff who can speak the languages and are familiar with these cultures to get involved in the transition process. As Britain is so cosmopolitan, it is likely that large companies would already have such resources within their own organisations if they looked carefully enough.

For people who are from minority cultures, climbing the ladder is often more difficult and they have to work three times as hard or be three times as smart to succeed. This is where discrimination surfaces – when one is smart and ambitious. The talent can lead to jealousy and fear among colleagues. If the contribution can be seen directly in terms of the difference it makes to the profits, then it may be difficult to hide, and bosses higher up may want such people to progress. However, if the organisational culture does not accommodate diversity, then it would stifle progression at some point or another. There have been cases where deliberate traps are laid to get rid of some unwanted people.

Culture Conflict

For large global organisations, differences in cultures can give rise to serious conflicts when they try to operate jointly or cooperate across borders. In such circumstances, inter-mediation and arbitration may be the only way forward. Otherwise, there would be senior-level departures of exec-utives, which organisations can ill-afford to lose. Although there are no statistics of such conflicts, we do know that they arise and can cause serious disruption.

The Chartered Institute of Personnel Development commissioned a major survey in 2006 of diversity in the business workplace. In all, 285 organisations were surveyed. The results indicate that the most important driver for diversity is 'legal pressure', with 68 per cent of the respondents ranking it among the top five drivers. Only around 17 per cent of the respondents reported the 'business case' as being the most important driver for diversity in their organisations. This suggests that the concept of diversity has not yet been fully grasped and businesses are not embracing the commercial and other benefits of diversity. There is still a way to go for companies to see diversity as a natural way of working and also as a commercial oppor-tunity.

There is also a difference in the legal obligations between working for a commercial organisation or a public sector organisation. Under the revised Race Relations Act of 2001, there are obligations for public bodies to be diverse, in terms of both recruitment and services. The same legal pressure and obligation does not apply to commercial organisations. At present, the Cabinet Office has set out a ten-point plan with targets for senior civil servants – 10 per cent of whom have to be from women and ethnic minorities by 2008. This is a serious strategic commitment to push diversity into the upper echelons of the Civil Service. Private organisations do not have any such explicit targets.

Public vs Private Sector

Cultures of public organisations and private organisations also vary. By definition, most public sector organisations operate within UK and are accountable locally. Rarely do they operate or trade internationally. Also, employment in public sector organisations is usually secure and protected, so to bring about cultural change is much slower. There is not the same pressure for performance and accountability as exists in commercial organisations. Also the structure of public organisations tends to be very hierarchical, and if the top is not diverse, it is unlikely to filter to the bottom. In the banking industry, which is a highly competitive and international business, especially in London, the diversity among employees is very visible. The competition means that employers have to seek the best talents irrespective of colour or creed and this results in diverse workplaces. This level of diversity is slowly seeping through to the top, but is not quite there yet.

Workplace Surveys

There have been surveys of diversity in the judiciary, academia, and public appointments in Scotland. All these surveys recognise that there is a problem, that numbers are not proportionate, nor are promotions proportionate. In the case of the judiciary, the survey report issued by Opinion Research Ltd in 2006 found that there was a feeling among many that the entire system is prejudiced and there is a strong resistance to diversity among some senior leaders of the profession. The report was an attempt by the government (Department of Constitutional Affairs) to discover what the problems were and how they could be rectified so that there was equality of access and progression for all. Another survey by the Association of University Teachers found that although 40 per cent of staff were women, their ranks were inversely proportional to the seniority of the grade – the more senior the grade, the lower the proportion of senior academics in that grade. They noted that there has been significant improvement in the number of women academics hired over the survey period. Unfortunately, there was no quality ethnic minority monitoring data for them to comment upon and in all there were 1.5 per cent of staff who were disabled.

Private sector organisations have hitherto been driven by profit as the sole commercial objective. This can mean that there is a homogenising influence, and profit dominates the organisational language – the focus is on financial return. Soft issues like culture, diversity and employee motivation may take a lower importance in such circumstances. The orientation can often be short-termist or material and people who are attracted by these values succeed in these organisations. In such cases, respect for different cultures and beliefs may be more superficial than real. There is a move nowadays toward corporate social responsibility and some large organisations are developing a range of objectives and taking their social responsibility more seriously. These are also the organisations likely to embrace diversity sincerely. So the ethos of the organisation in terms of its business ethics and long-term orientation makes a big difference to the environment it creates for diversity to flourish.

Set Ways

Workplaces are occupied by adults whose cultures and values have already been shaped in their childhood. They can also be internally competitive places, especially if the organisation structure is such that either you move up or you move out – there is no other way to progress. This internal competition can lead to intolerance and friction, even where colleagues are meant to work together to achieve a common goal. If cultural variety or disability is added to the space, the situation can be exacerbated. If, on the other hand, the organisation structure is such that individuals have a significant amount of empowerment and flexibility, there is a good chance that diversity will be tolerated and respected.

By definition, workplaces are also serious spaces, where there is little time and effort devoted to play and creativity, and a lot of energy devoted to providing goods and services. The larger an organisation, the more resistant it can be to change. The smaller an organisation, the easier it is for it to change and respond to new situations and problems. Size can have an impact on outlook and culture, but there can be large organisations which operate as a network of small organisations. This allows for greater creative freedom and opportunity for diversity to flourish.

The 2006 survey of the judiciary mentioned above found some startling evidence. People perceived the organisational culture to be closed and stereotypical, where in order to succeed and progress you had to fit in. There was little room for manoeuvre. Some legal professionals even felt that the entire legal system was against diversity and equality of opportunity, even though the laws promoted it. This is very surprising coming from a profession which is very influential in British society. Can the legal profession truly break the law against institutional racism? I have also heard from individuals who have had to rely on the legal process to obtain justice that they experienced serious difficulties if they were non-white. Thus the quality of service and justice received by British citizens varies depending on ethnicity.

External Forces

External forces can influence an organisation's culture significantly. One example is when there is a takeover by a foreign-owned company, as has happened to much of the car industry in this country. This can lead to a significant shift in methods of operation, especially if the new owner comes from a very different culture and mindset. In such a situation, attitudes and behaviour may have to change quickly, although there may be training to manage the transition.

When an organisation expands its operations abroad, it can be forced to incorporate diversity as it would be working with people from different cultures and delegating power and authority to them. This is happening increasingly as the world becomes smaller. There are trends in outsourcing and contracting to cheap labour countries like India and China, and this would necessitate the owners and managers to learn the different cultures, and vice versa. It may even lead to greater recruitment of Indian origin and Chinese origin people in the UK headquarters to help manage the expansion and transition.

The way in which BME businesses are managed is very diverse, depending very often on the ownership and the culture of the owners. I am a Gujarati Indian, and Gujaratis are regarded as some of the smartest businessmen and entrepreneurs. As a Jain by religion, it adds further to this strength, because there is strong culture of self-discipline which makes us natural leaders. Jain values require us to be sincere, hard-working, disciplined, dedicated and tolerant. Most books on leadership say that the common denominator for all leaders are values and integrity. Jains have an openness to new ideas and thinking, a desire and courage to go against the crowd and break new ground, and a strong work ethic. Family businesses are common amongst Gujaratis and there is strong support and sustenance which this provides, even through some of the most difficult times. Also being part of large organised social and community groups gives us access to significant social capital which we would not be able to tap otherwise.

In the UK, there are a large number of companies and businesses owned by ethnic minorities. Often, they start in this way because they cannot get a job so they do something on their own. Businesses like restaurants, newsagents, grocers and general supplies start in this way. Nowadays as the communities have matured and there is much better education, we also get professional businesses like accountants, solicitors, pharmacies and medical and dental practices which are owned and managed by ethnic minorities. Some of these have grown into large national chains like Sigma Pharmaceuticals or Nucare, for example, who are in the pharmaceutical industry.

Leadership

As many organisations are primarily hierarchical, leadership and the behaviour and outlook of the leaders has a huge impact on the culture of an organisation. The leaders' attitudes to diversity will depend on their own upbringing, ethnic background and experiences. If they have been raised in multicultural backgrounds and gone to school where there is a diversity of students and staff, then it is likely that their outlook will be different. If, on the other hand, they are brought up in predominantly white neighbourhoods and they do not have friends from ethnic minority backgrounds, then they are less likely to believe in diversity and emphasise its importance in the organisation. It is not enough for a leader today to say I do not believe in discrimination, so my organisation is OK. Positive pro-active steps need to be taken to embrace diversity and inculcate such values throughout the organisation.

There are very few organisations in the UK today which can be said to have such a culture. Just because an organisation appears as if its staff are varied and multi-ethnic may still not mean that it embraces diversity. For example, it depends on how many BME people are in senior positions in this organisation. It may be that they are hired to work for them but not allowed to share any power. At an extreme, it can mean that all the staff are forced to adapt to the mainstream organisational culture and those who do that are the ones who are hired.

One result of this pressure to fit in sometimes leads to the creation of 'coconuts' – people who are black or brown on the outside, but white inside. This is especially true for some coloured people who occupy senior positions in businesses and government. Coconuts are people who deliberately change their values and actions to try to climb the corporate ladder. The result of this may mean that they experience 'identity stress' later on in life and also sacrifice their personal family life to fulfil their ambitions.

Mentoring can be an effective way of retaining and promoting quality employees from minority backgrounds. It helps them to negotiate the difficult terrain and air their grievances, with constructive and creative support. A mentor who is in a senior position (in the same or a different organisation) from a similar cultural background can act as a listener when problems arise and can provide practical guidance as he/she has been through similar situations themselves. This is especially important in organisations which are steering a path of change from exclusivity to inclusivity and wish to improve diversity at all levels.

Monitoring Processes and Outcomes

Because of the legislation, there is a need to record and monitor processes of recruitment and promotion and ensure that there is fairness and equity at all levels. Managers have to attend courses on diversity and be fully conversant with their legal obligations. One way organisations circumvent the legislation on race discrimination is at the time of recruitment because it can be very difficult for applicants to prove that they have been discriminated against as they would not have the full facts about the quality of the other candidates. In my case, I have applied for public sector jobs where I felt sure I was the most qualified candidate and I have not received a letter of rejection – there is simply no written response. I know this also happens in relation to age discrimination. Old people generally cannot get jobs nowadays, especially if they are well qualified. However, if it is found that a large organisation has very few BME staff, then this can act against them, suggesting institutional racism, if there was ever a case on race discrimination. Either way, great care has to be taken by organisations in their employment practices.

Another area where the landscape is changing is supplier diversity. Organisations, especially public bodies, need to ensure that their suppliers operate diverse policies and recruit staff from diverse backgrounds. Large contracts to supply equipment or services are now being scrutinised and here again, there is commercial pressure to embrace diversity. Recently, Microsoft in the UK rejected a supplier because of the lack of diversity in its staffing. Companies may find that they lose the opportunity to win large contracts to supply to public organisations.

Whose dis-ability?

In terms of disability, workplaces are now legally obligated to have full disabled access. However, there is no statistical evidence of the percentages of disabled people in large public and private sector organisations. My fear is that as there is no legal obligation to have a certain minimum percentage, most organisations discriminate against hiring disabled employees. If and when they do hire them, I suspect that they are not able to climb the ladder of promotion and are not given the opportunity and training to progress. I see hardly any disabled executives anywhere. As a society, we have to question why this is so.

B&Q DIY chain have established a network of 300 partnerships between its stores and disability groups nationwide. The feeling is that 'if we get it right for disabled people, we can get it right for most people'. It has appointed staff disability champions for each store and has experienced an improvement in its brand image. Both B&Q and Sainsbury's have a policy of actively recruiting and training older age staff whom they find to be more stable and reliable and it is paying dividends for their productivity.

Disabled people are also as important a part of society as any other. In fact, there is criticism about the use of the term, because it implies that others are fully able somehow. In America, they use terms like 'physically challenged' to talk about physical disability, and 'mentally challenged' to talk about mental disability. In our culture, we believe that people who are weak in one area, have exceptional strengths in other areas to compensate for this weakness. Thus disabled people can be huge resources for organisations, if only they take the time and provide resources to nurture and support them in the early years and give them the right mix of opportunities. They could give them the best loyalty, and also give staff a subtle message that all are equal and worthy of respect.

Women and Seniority

Even for women, the law is very clear – there should be equality of opportunity and prospects. In recent years, there has been a major change in the percentages of women in senior positions, but it is still nowhere near a proportionate representation. There are also issues relating to discrepancies of pay, with women earning less in the same positions than their male counterparts. This is illegal.

One of the key issues facing women is support and understanding when they choose to have children. Very few organisations have effective policies which support them during this time and enable them to continue their career progression and training. Often, women are asked to choose between work and home and they end up taking career breaks, which make it difficult for them to return to work after a few years. Certainly jobs are never frozen for them. This does seriously affect their progression and partly explains why the percentage of women in senior positions is still low today. For organisations to facilitate such schemes, they need to have a longer term orientation and value the diversity in the workforce and give equality of opportunity to all. The fact that women do not get good support suggests that there are very few organisations which genuinely respect their talents and contribution to society.

The increasing emphasis on corporate social responsibility comes from the philosophy that corporations are also citizens of the countries in which they operate, and like all citizens, they carry rights and responsibilities. One of these responsibilities is to care for the society and the workforce in which they operate. Firms should work in a way which is sustainable and not oriented towards short-term greed and profit-maximisation. If organisations genuinely believe in this, then diversity becomes a natural part of how they operate and support their employees and serve their customers.

Creative Bridge-Building

One of my friends, Mr Satish Kanabar, is a senior banker in

London and Director of Barclays (West London Corporate Team) who really believes in community service. He gets directly involved in local charities, not just for fund-raising but also giving hands-on support to local schools and communities. Every year, his team organises a multi-faith Christmas/Diwali/Eid festival party for customers which is entirely devoted to charity and the funds raised are given to a local charity and matched by the bank. This is a good example of corporate social responsibility and all the staff get really motivated and empowered to make this event happen. By celebrating all the various festivals in one event, he is also embracing diversity and saying to everyone that they are welcome and he is grateful for their business throughout the year. How often do we hear organisations publicly thanking their customers for their support? Furthermore, for the customers (many of whom are entrepreneurs themselves and leaders of large organisations) it gives a really good message of corporate social responsibility and encourages them to do likewise – he sets a good example for others as well.

Last year, I received a Christmas Greetings Card from the Chief Executive of the Centre for Excellence in Leadership, Ms Lynne Sedgmore CBE, who seriously believes in diversity and pro-actively pushes it up the agenda for her own and connected organisations in higher education. There is a group photo of all the staff in the card and it is very diverse and multicultural. I have rarely seen an organisation with such diversity. They practice what they preach. Their website is also very diverse and has a Faith Toolkit which is one of the most popular downloads. It demonstrates to me very clearly that diversity is possible here and now and can be a source of strength and resilience.

What I see often, however, is that many organisations

and leaders have an unwritten philosophy – especially those who are commercially oriented. The policy is: 'Not in my back yard'. In an article in the *Guardian* newspaper (dated 17 June 2006), there was a story about Neana Lawson who was visually impaired and applied for a job in a large computer firm. She emailed them to say that she needed more time to do the test because of her disability. They responded in January to her email, after the application deadline had passed. So there was no job chance for her, in a company which declared itself to have an equal opportunities policy. Many employers do not want to do anything or lack the patience to allow disabled people to flower and bloom. It is also likely that they will and are getting away with this subtle discrimination. But they need to be careful, because if they are sued under the new legislation, they can get into trouble for rejecting job applications on grounds of disability.

Thus when organisations genuinely believe in equality of opportunity for all, they can and do make a difference. They also get a huge return for their efforts. It creates a workforce which is fulfilled, and this comes out in their output and productivity. It is a win-win situation for all. The organisation does not rely on legislation to push it to action. It does it because it believes in equality and fairness for all and has a deeper sense of social responsibility and accountability. It cares and believes, and acts accordingly. There is integrity.

CHAPTER SUMMARY

- Not all workplaces are diverse.
- Even where there is diversity, there may not be equivalent seniority.

- Leadership has an influence on organisational cultures. In Britain, leaders are very often white and male.
- There is evidence of institutional racism in some organisations. Here, attitudes and structures are fundamentally racist.
- Genuine diversity across the organisation needs to be supported and nurtured.
- Minorities of all kinds can be threatened by majorities and their progress restricted.
- Organisations can have common values and uncommon cultures, if there is respect for one another. They are expected to monitor the diversity and rank of employees within the organisation.
- Mentoring support is very helpful to minorities who wish to climb the ladder but often find the journey lonely and unsupported.
- It is a social responsibility and duty of organisations to provide equality of opportunity to all and now also a legal obligation.
- Hierarchical organisations have a particular problem with accommodating diversity.

POINTS TO PONDER

- How diverse is your workplace?
- Are there equal opportunities at time of recruitment and in terms of training, experience and promotion?
- In what ways can you build bridges of understanding through creativity and imagination?
- Is there training and mentoring available?

- What is the culture of the organisation – is it hierarchical or is it open and democratic?
- When conflicts arise, how are they resolved?
- If yours is an international organisation, is there an attempt to understand the cultures of the partners?

Love Thy Neighbour

Home is where the heart is. Home is where families extend into communities. Home is where we connect and share with one another and our children embark on their futures. It is the art studio with a living pallette. How we choose to live can make all the difference to our common future.

Where is the Community?

Research commissioned by the RSA (Royal Society of Arts) in 2006 found that more than two-thirds of people surveyed (68 per cent) admitted that they did not take part in any local community activity. Many people aren't even prepared to strike up a conversation with those they run into on a day-to-day basis: 49 per cent said they wouldn't do so in their local shop, and 87 per cent wouldn't go out of their way to chat to someone at the school gates. In spite of this, more than half the people surveyed (53 per cent) said that they would probably feel happier and more connected if they did participate in the locality. Experts labelled this phenomenon 'Community Detachment Syndrome'.

During the Queen's Golden Jubilee, a few of us got together to organise a street party in our neighbourhood in Colchester. An informal committee was set up, ideas were taken from everyone, roles and responsibilities were delegated and games and events were planned. The actual day turned out to be dry and because we live in a close, the party was safe on the street. It was one of the first times that neighbours came out of their 'shells' and relaxed and chilled out. Otherwise, it is a quick wave and smile as we are rushing to work or to school. Sadly, the effect of the party did not last long and everyone retreated back into their lives very quickly.

Unfortunately, in our hectic world, neighbours often remain as strangers. Also, mainstream British culture is a private culture, and there is a feeling that neighbours want to preserve their privacy and not engage 'too much'. Closeness can become messy and cumbersome, and it is better to keep one's safe distance. Hence we do not live in a commune-ity. We live in clusters of homes called communities. There is little that is common between us, except for our busy-ness and selfishness. Often we are transient, moving homes regularly and allowing no time for us to settle down and connect with the locality. Not all of these movements are in our control – our employers or jobs may force us to move about. So how can we love our neighbours? One of the Ten Commandments is: Love thy neighbour as thyself. If we do not love our neighbours, do we really love ourselves? Perhaps it is because we do not love our deeper inner selves that we do not love our neighbours. Instead we love our material or physical selves, which are impermanent and will die sooner or later.

Strange Neighbours

And what of diversity in our neighbourhoods? That becomes an even remoter issue, and it is possible that colour or difference can make our neighbours even more strange. There may be moments when we have to encounter one another, say when we pick up our kids from the same school, or we share a fence which needs repairing. Then we have to communicate and break our 'privacy'. Otherwise, it is comfortable staying private. That way we do not have to trust anyone but ourselves. We can be left alone to be alone. In my experience, it is rare for ethnic minorities to get any special welcome when they move into a white neighbourhood. As always, 'they' are expected to fit in.

If we have children, then they will change the landscape – given a chance. They will start talking to neighbours. My son sometimes goes into a home if the door is opened without being invited because he is raised in a culture where we visit relatives and friends at their homes, and we don't always need to be invited to do so. Children will often make friends with other children and bring the parents to talk to one another. They will help 'create' a neighbourhood. If we deny them this opportunity, then we will be giving similar signals to them when they grow up. Life is about privacy, keeping your doors closed and keeping your distance. You only get together if you are invited. Neighbours can be a nuisance.

In the schools or shopping malls, we will encounter people who live locally. We may have to sit next to them at a nativity play or during a local fete. We may bump into them in a shopping centre, whilst carrying our shopping. Here there is no time for idle talk because we are probably rushing to get to the car park or make sure we complete our shopping list. Local shops have all but closed down and have been replaced by large car park superstores. This is the life we live today – and the stresses are real for many. For those who are super-rich, there are no neighbours. The houses are far apart and the privacy is fully secured. There seem to be different secluded worlds for them.

Yet on the news and radio, I keep hearing this word 'community'. I ask myself: Where is it? Who creates it, nurtures it and sustains it? Is it a word which the media has promoted to describe people living in a common area, a soundbite summary for a collection of strangers? Can communities really exist in this modern jetset world of transience and insecurity? The local authorities have to deal with residents and good communities can save them money and resources because they will have mutual support networks. Weak communities will remain a burden on the councils, requiring all kinds of services and support from health to crime prevention, drug abuse, and poverty alleviation.

Good Examples

Diversity and equality require us to respect our neighbours, irrespective of their colour, sexuality, ability or creed. For this to happen, we need to acknowledge their presence, organise and participate in shared events, even go to each other's houses. Most of the neighbourhood connections happen through schools or any local clubs we may be part of, like a library reading group or a sports club. If we send our children to faraway private schools, then even these connections get broken. If we belong to any communities, these may be distant rather than local. It seems that we have fewer chances of meeting.

The Royal Society of Arts in cooperation with Starbucks started the 'Coffeehouse Challenge' in 2004 to encourage locals to come together and discuss the issues in a focused way. There is no definite commitment or endgame required, but surprisingly, many things which start off as discussions, end up in very successful community renewal or regeneration projects taken up by the local members. For example, on the island of Angelsey, Mr Colin Hawkins with other locals decided to do something about the youth problem because they had nowhere to go to meet one another and do activities together. So they decided to set up a digilab where the youth could make music or creative photos and print them. They were facilitated to create their own management team by the adults and encouraged to run the centre in their own way. This is a good example of how local engagement can lead to transformation. Such a facility is open to all youth, irrespective of their culture, beliefs or disability.

Another excellent example of community building is the Wilson Marriage Learning Centre in Colchester where I live. Here, people from all ages, cultures and abilities or disabilities regularly come to learn, create, share and connect with one another. Mrs Pat Nunn, who heads the centre recently took me on a tour there, and she showed me the lift that they had just installed. She was very proud of it. This means that there is full access to the upper floors for disabled people. The in-house cafe serves fresh food and hot drinks at very reasonable prices for the students and visitors and there is a real sense of community spirit in this space. It is especially popular among all kinds of minorities – a place where diversity is truly practised without it being a statement or a regulation. The organisation believes in it and encourages all kinds of community initiatives. When we approached them to start a Saturday Gujarati School for our children, they went out of their way to find us a good space and give us all the support we needed. We received constant compliments about the politeness and good behaviour of our children. They also host a nursery and day care space for disabled children run by a charity called 'Stepping Stones'. This is a huge respite for the carers of this children and the charity provides a priceless service which is not available anywhere else.

In London or Leicester, communities are diverse by nature. People have no choice but to live in mixed neighbourhoods – generally speaking. There are some exceptions of ghetto areas occupied either by the very rich or the very poor which can be mono-cultural. Whereas half a century ago, owners used to say 'no blacks, dogs or Irish' outside their homes, this is just not possible today and few city estate agents can afford to operate under such restrictions. Even in exclusive rich areas, there can be exclusive BME people who have the money to afford such big houses. So in cosmopolitan cities, diversity becomes part of the very fabric of life and increasingly becomes a core strength. The schools are very cosmopolitan, although there are areas where whites can be a minority at school.

Are We All Semi-Detached?

If residents do not directly engage in community building, then the burden of community regeneration falls onto the local authorities. Here, there seems to be great diversity as to how the councils approach these matters within regions and localities. The Department of Communities and Local Government has been set up to spearhead a drive towards 'community cohesion'. There is a positive and pro-active attempt to help build, nurture and sustain lasting communities. Some local authorities are more pro-active than others, and give attention and resources to diversity and community infrastructure. However, there is always a limit to how much councils can do and it is up to residents to build and nurture communities. At most, they can create a positive space and facilities for communities to grow.

One quality that is a key ingredient to building lasting local communities is trust. We must have some grain of trust to begin with and it can grow as we get to know one another. Without trust, we will remain isolated, selfish and live very detached lives. This is why children are so central to building communities. They start with innocence and have a natural trust and respect for everyone irrespective of their colour or background. Good local public playgrounds and other children's facilities therefore become key building blocks for communities. The more relaxed the children are, the more relaxed their parents will be and they will strike up conversations with one another at the playground or school yard.

Valuing Community

There also needs to be an appreciation of the value of good communities. In the modern world where money is a common currency, many feel that there is no need for communities at all. Money can buy anything that they need and hence there is no need to rely on anyone or to trust anyone – we can all trust money instead. There is a famous quote by Margaret Thatcher when she was Prime Minister: 'There is no such thing as "society"'. This is clearly not true if we look at a neighbourhood in the longer term and it can only be sustained by people who are somehow connected to one another. Money can create the illusion of independence, but in truth it is only that – an illusion. We need one another. The government and local authorities provide us with services such as education, healthcare, security and cleanliness, and this removes a significant part of our burden of social responsibility. However, this cannot remove our need to respect and trust one another.

Sacrifice is a key part of community building. It means giving up some of our time and resources to help others locally. There is no direct measurable return for this. However, there are many indirect benefits from this which are often not understood or experienced by many. Giving time enables us to experience service and the joy of self-lessness. It also connects us to others because we are helping them and have no expectation in return. It creates an atmosphere of trust and friendship. It also sets an example to our children, who do it naturally. But when they see their parents doing it, they feel encouraged and grow up learning that community service is a social duty. No one asks us to sacrifice all our time and neglect our jobs or families – we just need to give up a small part of that time on a regular basis.

Joy of Giving

I have done this very naturally and routinely for over two decades in this country and have really enjoyed it and learnt hugely from it. One thing that it also does is to put a check on our own greed and materialism, reminding us of the limits of money. We come to know a large number of people through this, and they come to know us. Remember that most people like to be helped, and we will make friends across all ranks and positions. Volunteering creates a spirit of equality and it does not matter whether we are a manager or an executive, when we volunteer and work collectively for a common goal. It is true that there are some people who are very proud and refuse to take help from others and sometimes they are even suspicious of the motives of others who wish to help them. This is sad and will not help us build lasting communities. We need to learn to be able to receive gracefully as well as give gracefully and there is no harm in receiving.

To educate people about my culture, I offered a 'Spirit of India' seminar series, with topics as varied as India itself – art, history and geography, pilgrimage and faith, Bollywood, food and festivals, and finally, liberation. I used a variety of techniques and resources including film clips, pictures, sounds and direct experience of festivals to convey the message. Throughout this project, my whole family was directly involved, with my son Meerav looking after the IT and projection, my daughter Jaina helping me to prepare the topics and my wife organising the welcome party and the food and dress sessions. We also organised a one-day coach trip entitled 'Pilgrimage to India in Britain' visiting the Jain, Hindu and Sikh temples. This was a creative exercise in bridge-building which was offered at a very low cost so that it would be accessible to all.

Nurturing Trust

Where there is a communal atmosphere, it becomes easier to exchange telephone numbers and email addresses and trust is nurtured. We can start to exchange information about local suppliers and services, which doctor or dental surgery is the nearest and best, and so on. The pace at which such relationships grow depends on our own mutual interest and willingness, but what it does do is to build a connection with the local people. It may even mean that people would be reluctant to move from one town to another if they have put down some roots and built friendships. Otherwise, transience becomes a norm and trust is never created or experienced.

We are fortunate in the UK to have many public institutions to bring us closer together – like libraries, schools, public parks, theatres and museums and art galleries. Many of these services are free or subsidised and very useful for our personal growth, well-being and development. They are open to all and do not discriminate among their visitors and users.

Sadly, I find often that some people just do not know what is happening locally and have little connection because all they do is use the services provided by local authorities but do not participate in anything. They may be busy with their work commitments and spend all their time at weekends resting and recovering from a busy week. This is especially true of parents with young children. Here, my advice would be to do some volunteering with the children so that the precious family time continues, but in a larger shared atmosphere. Of course this is not easy for people who are genuinely living at the edge and working all hours just to survive.

Inequality

There is also inequality between the givers and the non-givers. Those who give voluntarily of their time and services give a lot and routinely, because they really believe in it. My daughter's saxophone teacher refuses to take money for his coaching – so we give him some food instead. He believes that there are some things in life which should not be bought or sold for money – and knowledge is one of them. This is not the only volunteering he does as he also works for the Co-op and organises social events regularly for members to come together. On the other hand, those who do not volunteer, do not give any of their time at all to any organisations. Hence they rarely experience the 'benefits' of volunteering and mistrust people who give freely of their time for having ulterior motives.

It is possible to widen participation and involvement by educating people about the benefits of volunteering. I know friends who have never done this before in their whole life and genuinely do not know how to participate and get involved. It is not that they do not want to do it – they have just not experienced the joy of participation and the possibilities for learning and engagement it can give them. Perhaps this is a role that the councils can take on in an innovative way so that communities come together. Also those who are volunteers should nurture them by 'holding their hands' in the early days so that they can experience for themselves the benefits of participation.

Schools, Charities and Faith Communities

There are a few major institutions in this country that can and do build and nurture communities: schools, charities and faith organisations. Schools bring people of all cultures and beliefs living in a neighbourhood together through the education of their children. Charities and clubs bring people together on the platform of helping others who are less fortunate. Faith-based organisations bring people together through their faith and they may come from far to meet one another during major festivals and celebrations. By its very nature, faith inspires community. This is a strength which is often forgotten and under-played by the secularist journalists and media.

Some examples are appropriate here. The Brahmakumaris are an excellent faith-based organisation in the UK with a national network of branches and headquarters in London. They regularly conduct free workshops and outreach programmes which integrate faith with everyday life and target, in particular, young people, the elderly and any individuals who need help and support. Every Christmas, they prepare a unique pantomime which is open to the public and they do special performances for children from schools in the locality where they are based in Willesden, North London. As a result of this, they have been accepted as a part of the neighbourhood in a very positive way and people have a very high respect for their work. They show, through lived example, the importance of good communities and neighbourliness, and love all their neighbours and welcome them to their centre. They do not discriminate between caste or creed and are very open and accessible. Even though they are a charity, it is their policy not to charge for a single course, seminar or event. In 2007, they organised a huge JAM (Just-A-Minute) at the Wembley Arena which was very innovative and again brought together people from all over London to learn about the benefits of spirituality and have fun at the same time. Among their guest performers was Mr Robin Gibb of the Bee Gees!

Churches also bring people together and there are thousands of churches of many traditions throughout the United Kingdom. Frequent services mean that members meet and pray together on a regular basis and it is a collective act. The same happens in churches, synagogues, mosques, temples or gurudwaras. At these meetings, people forget their work-a-day struggles and focus on the divine and what is common and binds them together. For many, these gatherings give them an identity and sense of purpose which helps them to live life to the full and cope with the ups and downs of human existence. It helps nurture their inner strength and self-confidence.

The emphasis on diversity by faith groups varies from one group to another. Some are conservative and fixated on the right way of doing things which has passed down through generations. Others in contrast are much more open and flexible, willing to discover new ways of doing old things and reinventing them to appeal to young people and newer congregations. They are dynamic and able to stay connected with the changing times and issues facing their members. Interfaith groups have now sprung up nationally to enable people to learn about other faiths and respect differing traditions and beliefs. Such groups help to build bridges and help promote and sustain diversity.

Unfortunately, membership of faith organisations by young people is in decline. There is an image that it is uncool to be religious. Young people need some identity to replace this and seek it in music, friends and sometimes escapism like drugs or alcohol. In this way, they often lose their connection with the neighbourhoods and local communities where they come from and this has an impact when they grow up and start their own families.

Schools are special in the sense that all who live within a certain geographical boundary are guaranteed a place in the school. Thus there is no discrimination at the point of entry, except that one has to be able to afford a house in that locality. The children make friends with one another and start inviting each other for their birthday parties. Also there are parent meetings at school and a parent-teacher association in every school, designed to engage parents in the running of the school and get their help in organising fund-raising events like school fetes or Christmas bazaars. Furthermore, many parents (usually mothers) are helpers in the classroom, assisting with reading, special needs and general teacher support. I know that whenever I have gone to my children's schools, either to help or to do an assembly, the children give me a special buzz which I cannot find anywhere else.

Never Makes the News, but Still Makes a Difference

In terms of promoting diversity and connectivity, state schools can do a unique job by bringing all kinds of people together and not giving any special attention to their culture or faith. Often they add to this by celebrating festivals and involving parents from particular cultures and faiths to participate and share in their experience. In this way, the school facilitates education and awareness of different cultures and beliefs to young developing minds and removes the veil of ignorance. Whenever my wife Nina has done Diwali or dressing up events with young children, the Indian colours and clothes are a smash hit and the whole class has a ball. This is low-key bridge building which will never make the news, but definitely makes a difference. Even the teachers learn about diversity in this way and experience the richness of having parents from different cultures within the school community. Hopefully their teaching also evolves through such activities and engagement.

Other organisations such as Rotary, Lions, Round Table, and Scouts also bring people together in a non-partisan way. They are often run and managed by volunteers with the sole purpose of fulfilling a charitable goal. For some, they provide a badge of identity and a value system which they identify with and connect with at a deeper level. Whatever the motive, such organisations connect different types of people to one another, people who would not otherwise meet or get to know one another. They help to break barriers and promote community cohesion.

Neighbourhood Design

We also need to look at the design and building of our housing complexes and spaces. For example, in most of the new apartment blocks that are being built, there is no common room or space where neighbours can have a casual chat. The result is that we have anonymous residents who live side by side, but are private and sometimes even afraid to smile at neighbours. If we cannot have a community in an apartment block, where people are living in one shared building, then where can we have people respecting one another?

The design of our community spaces and neighbourhoods can also make a difference to our connectedness. Traditionally in Britain, the pub was a very important 'local community centre', where people regularly went to relax and connect with one another. Nowadays however, that has fragmented much more, and in towns, there are also lots of wine bars and other places where people can go to have a drink. Very few pubs in towns have a regular loyal clientele and in fact many are closing down or being forced to reinvent themselves.

Parks and children's playgrounds are also important communal spaces, and they are often within walking distance from homes. Unfortunately, they suffer from the problem of vandalism and their facilities lack creativity. The amount of money spent on these by councils seems to be relatively low. Parks are beautiful natural spaces and their bio-diversity encourages human diversity and respect. Engagement and dialogue happens between dogs or children, and then the adults will communicate. Rarely does it happen directly. It is possible that when builders request permission for new housing complexes, they are required to build communal multi-faith spaces where residents from all faiths and none can meet and engage with one another, or just pray together in silence. The tent at St Ethelburga's which I mentioned earlier would make a good model example for this. It would also be a positive space for children to grow up in a place where the sacred is not distant but a part of everyday life. But all this requires imagination, and when looking at the huge amount of new building that is going on in Britain, it seems to lack that one quality and the entire focus is on profit. Of course if the planning laws were to require it, then the situation can be different. It is certainly worth trying to build creative communal spaces which attract people to come together and connect.

If we are to really build community cohesion, the culture of privacy in Britain needs to change. We need to find a way of trusting one another and having a dialogue in our neighbourhoods. Engaging with people need not be a blot on our privacy, nor is it really an infringement on theirs. Common causes such as education and peaceful neighbourhoods should serve to bring us together. All of us should make efforts to have some local friends with whom we socialise and do things together and this will help us connect to the locality and also educate our children about the importance of local friendships. Otherwise, we will remain temporary migrants in our own country with no loyalty to any physical or natural space. This can create a continuous restlessness.

CHAPTER SUMMARY

- Neighbourhoods and communities are breaking apart all over Britain.

- We lack a shared purpose and sense of belonging. We give too much emphasis to privacy and too little to social cohesiveness.

- Few people see it as their duty to support and cultivate good communities.

- A healthy neighbourhood creates a healthy community, which leads to a healthy nation.
- Diversity can enrich the neighbourhood, although often it is not allowed to do so.
- Public organisations like schools, parks, churches, libraries and museums and art galleries help to bring people together.
- Children are excellent bridge-builders, but often do not have the power to influence change.
- Creative neighbourhood spaces are great ways of getting people together to communicate and share.

POINTS TO PONDER

- Do you realise the value of a good neighbourhood?
- Would you like to give some time to building, supporting and nurturing your local community?
- How do you welcome minorities in your neighbourhood?
- Can local engagement help your personal fulfilment and give meaning and purpose to your life?
- Think of what you like and enjoy doing and how you can do so in a local community setting. Try and experience it for yourself.
- Don't be afraid of talking to adults and smiling with them.
- Be the change you wish to see in the world. It is easy to be cynical but much more fun to do our own bit for society. Involve the family in the process and you may be surprised by the results you can achieve.

Media and Communication

Rarely do we encounter diversity on a daily basis. We spend most of our time at home or at work, and even this time is limited to our immediate colleagues. Hence we live and work in cocoons, which do not reflect the cosmopolitan world around us. However, the time we spend listening to the radio, reading a newspaper, watching television or browsing the net can significantly influence our view of the world. The average Briton spends a staggering 20 hours a week watching television – let alone listening to the radio or reading a paper. If the news tells us that Muslims are to be watched as they could be potential terrorists, we become fearful and guarded. This becomes 'our' truth. If on the other hand, it tells us that most Muslims are peace loving and that there are only a few exceptions, then we may act differently toward Muslims. Often, the impact is subtle and subconscious, and we may not even realise that our views have been altered.

Very Influential

The media is a multi-billion-pound industry which is hugely influential. It is also thinly regulated. The only limited power or control we as individuals have on the media is through our pocket. A newspaper cannot directly influence us if we do not buy it. However, it can and does influence those who buy it, so if such people beat us for no reason other than that we are black, we are still affected by the paper. Fortunately, the BBC is a publicly owned broadcaster and as taxpayers, we do have an influence on its content.

Most people do not understand this industry and how it works – how it sometimes manufactures truth. For example, the editorial process which is applied prior to the final showing of a documentary or news item is huge. Sometimes, 40 hours of film would be reduced to 45 minutes of broadcast documentary film by the editor. It is the editors who do this selection. Also, whilst we see journalists appearing on radio or TV, the editors are often invisible and often unaccountable. It is here that our perceptions and world-views are shaped. It is also here that diversity can be manipulated or inadvertently tainted. The time restrictions of squeezing a news story into a few soundbites are such that the truth can be unwittingly distorted even though millions will consume this news story.

Colour Blind?

Advertising is a major component of modern media. How much of a newspaper is advertising, or what proportion of time in a half-hour TV slot is devoted to advertising? It can be up to 50 per cent and sometimes even more. Billboards, posters, radio – wherever we go, we are hit by advertising whether we like it or not. It is a multi-million-pound industry hiring some of the smartest creative talent. Underlying these adverts are subtle messages about culture and values which affect our subconscious perceptions. Many studies have shown that advertising promotes a consumer culture where we constantly feel inept and somehow ugly or unfulfilled, and we need to buy more to fulfil ourselves. As advertisements are commercially driven, they are not obligated to promote diversity and equality.

In fact, how often have you seen disabled people in an advertisement or ethnicity being portrayed for its richness rather than as a possible consumer? Some argue that advertising homogenises us, making us all look and feel similar so that we can be sold standard products at standard prices. Its aim is to quell diversity rather than to promote it. It does all this in a subtle and subliminal way.

Most editors of popular media are white males, especially of the powerful media, like *The Daily Mail, The Mirror, The Times, The Guardian, The Telegraph* or *The Financial Times.* Also most commercial media are businesses first, second and third. Hence their primary goal is to profit rather than to be authentic, honest or truthful. From the above, *The Guardian* is the only exception because it is owned by a trust and is not a private commercial company. If they can make a lot of money from doing a morally decadent programme, the media will do it. They do not care about the moral degradation of society, merely about profits, audience figures and advertising revenues. As such, there is no major obligation to promote diversity by the commercial media and they will only do so if it makes commercial sense.

In January 2007, Britain experienced a national debate on racism when an Indian contestant on the Channel 4 programme *Celebrity Big Brother*, Shilpa Shetty, was verbally abused on live television. This created a public storm, with a record 40,000 complaints from viewers to the media regulator, OFCOM. Here was news being created and shaped by the media. Even MPs complained about this as Channel 4 gets a major public grant and has accountability, and is supposed to cater for minority audiences. There was no public apology initially from the channel, which actually saw its ratings shoot up dramatically due to the controversy. Eventually, Shilpa Shetty won and became a major British celebrity in a very short time. Channel 4's argument was that by encouraging a national debate, it helped people come to see discrimination and also the beauty or lack of it of different cultures and peoples. The public issue is that racism should not be condoned by any media and is illegal.

The BBC is different from most media in that it is a totally publicly owned broadcaster and is closely regulated. This is also why its quality is often (though not always) so much better than that of other media. It has an obligation to be fair and accurate. There was a very famous announcement by the former Director General of the BBC, Mr Greg Dyke, who said publicly in 2001: 'The BBC is hideously white.' He admitted that the organisation's management structure was more than 98 per cent white and said that it was unable to retain staff from ethnic minorities and questioned if they were made to feel welcome. He also acknowledged that a failure of the corporation's equal opportunities policies was most noticeable at the highest levels. This is shocking for an organisation which has such a huge influence on British media and the British public.

Print Media

A 2005 survey by the Commission for Racial Equality in the print media sector in London also found equally shocking evidence. The researchers discovered the industry to be white male dominated, with a very small proportion of BME journalists. Those that did get jobs soon found themselves to be lonely and isolated, often leaving as a result. Some said that the sector is institutionally racist and diminishing of the achievements and aspirations of BME staff. Some ex-journalists felt that challenging editors or bosses about their racism would mark them as trouble-makers, making it impossible to find work elsewhere in the industry. The only area where there was a significant proportion of BME workers was in low-paid, low-status occupations like cleaning and catering. Also, as the quality jobs were based on class and contacts, BME journalists felt doubly disadvantaged as they had neither the colour nor the class and contacts to get up the career ladder into quality jobs.

Thus if the manufacturers of truth are biased, what is the impact on truth itself? And if truth is distorted, and this falsehood is consumed by the masses, the impact on our attitudes to diversity and respect for different cultures is very adverse and significant. At best, our views and knowledge will be influenced by stereotypical perceptions and at worst, readers or viewers will believe that ours is the only best culture and all 'foreigners' are either suckers or parasites who have nothing to give to Britain. This would lead to greater tension and segregation of the population and take us away from moving forward in this global village.

As a Jain, I was conscious of the enormous media influence and wanted to ensure that Jain culture had some space within it. I started working voluntarily with the BBC, helping the Head of Religion and Ethics, Mr Alan Bookbinder, visit different faith centres in the UK. He helped set up a Jainism section on the BBC website and introduced us to various journalists in the team. This was a major achievement for us, in spite of the fact that we were such a small community and little-known faith. I ended up chairing the Hindu/Jain advisory committee to BBC Religion and Ethics after three years of building and nurturing this relationship. In this way, the coverage of

Jain/Hindu culture improved and was sensitive to the needs of the community. I personally did several programmes on Radio 4 and BBC World Service and even helped the development of other programmes.

In general, the media is perceived as an insecure, competitive and aggressive industry to work for. It also attracts quality applicants because journalism is seen as a fun and challenging profession. By definition, cultures are complex, subtle and have taken thousands of years to grow and evolve. Hence to understand them and write about them in a manner which is culturally sensitive is very difficult, although not impossible. For an industry which is so slippery and with such a low attention span, the positive portrayal of culture therefore becomes structurally paralysed. There is no time to investigate or to be authentic and sensitive in the rush to produce, print and sell. All that is needed are people who can write good English and report under time pressure and in soundbites, making the news entertaining and enjoyable. Even if BME people are employed, the structures in place make it difficult to portray diversity in a sensitive way.

Change on the Horizon

As the law in this country has changed to stamp out institutional racism, since 2001 there is a much greater awareness about the public duty to promote equality and diversity. And the media has become sensitised to this and is doing much more than it has ever done before, especially the BBC. On radio and television, we are now increasingly seeing all kinds of faces and people, including disabled people appearing prominently. For example, there is a whole new BBC Asian Network on radio and the internet which is well resourced and covers the Asian diaspora nationally. There are a large number of private radio stations which cater to ethnic audiences. Local radio and television are bound by diversity legislation and they are also having to change their staff composition and media coverage to reflect ethnic diversity and equality. Even commercial media has changed, with Channel 4 becoming the most progressive of TV stations, embracing diversity not as a legal obligation but as a commercial opportunity – believing in it and portraying it in a positive way through a variety of programmes and series.

The job of an editor is to decide on the scope and depth of a programme, and the angle covered by the story. To be able to do this well, an editor needs to understand the context of a problem well, and how it would be defined and expressed in different cultures and belief systems. Ideally, a good editor should have a basic understanding of different cultures and belief systems. Otherwise, the way the editor filters a particular news or factual story will be biased by their own culture and belief systems.

For example, arranged marriages are a very common stereotypical question faced by Indians in Britain. For us, it seems odd that the first things people remember are the negative connotations. Furthermore, there is a huge variety of ways in which marriages are arranged and this process cannot be looked at without understanding our culture. Many of these methods are very liberal and modern and they actually facilitate marriages and many see them as a boon. In Indian culture, a marriage is not just between individuals but between families also, and it helps if the families can get along well too. This family support continues well after the marriage. Statistics show that arranged marriages are much more likely to survive over the long term than 'love' marriages. However, the stereotype and the taint remains.

Given that key influence is held by editors, how do we ensure that editors understand diversity and embrace it, allowing it to be portrayed positively and sensitively? Firstly, editors need to travel, watch, observe and engage with different cultures and communities. This is critical. Only when they see this world will they be able to act with responsibility and sensitivity. They need to hire editorial staff who are well trained in different cultures and come from diverse backgrounds. This will mean that if there is a breaking news story, there is at least one insider with whom it can be discussed to ensure cultural sensitivity in its portrayal. Processes of filtration and editing need to be carefully designed to allow for diverse content and presentation. Unfortunately, all the editors I know are super-busy and have very little time for engaging directly with the public and news stories.

Communicating in English

Language is a major barrier as all modern media in this country are primarily written or communicated in English. This means that even different cultures need to be expressed in English. Science has demonstrated very clearly that language and culture are deeply entwined, and it is very difficult to talk about a culture in a different language. For example, a classic confusion is with the word 'religion'. In Hindu and Jain tradition, the word used is 'Dharma', which translated into English would mean 'the science of sustainable living'. However, it is not wrong to refer to it as religion as it is about the sacred and the spiritual, but is not religion in the institutionalised Christian sense. Thus the translation becomes misleading and loses the significant difference that exists. This is especially serious if media editors perceive the eastern traditions in this way as they really misunderstand them and thereby misrepresent them or do not give them the authentic coverage.

Not only does a culture need to be expressed in English, it also needs to be done with clarity, sharpness and accuracy. For example, the *Today* programme on BBC Radio 4 is well known for its sharp and incisive journalism. If you are questioned on the programme, you need to understand the question clearly, and respond in a focused and accurate way instantaneously. As a result, only those who are fluent in this way can appear, even though they may not be the best commentators on a subject. On another similar programme, *Question Time*, I have constantly looked out for ethnic minority panellists and they are few and far between, probably for this reason – the editors want people who can respond quickly and accurately. For someone from a different culture to appear, not only do they need to know and understand their own culture well, they need to be able to articulate it and express it in a way which is understandable to a contemporary audience. This is not easy by any means. However, some of the best speakers on this programme for me have been from ethnic minority backgrounds.

Another example is the range of cooking programmes which are so popular today. I know that so far as many Jains are concerned, there is a master chef in every home. However, if you were to ask how many of them are capable of a positive media persona or even to explain their cooking styles and preferences in English on radio, then we would generally struggle. It seems frustrating that the media has no patience, because it is missing out on so much. These master chefs can make 365 different varied and delicious vegetarian meals in a year, and actually do practise it quietly and consistently in their homes without any fanfare. For them, cooking is a means to nourish the soul, not to becoming a celebrity or an art form worthy of display. In my opinion, they are the real chefs we should be celebrating, but it is unlikely they will ever get their deserved audience.

Celebrity Diversion

There is a lot of coverage given to celebrities in the media today. Very rarely do we find this celebrity focus to be based on culture or belief. Usually it is based on beauty or artistic skill. Often, it is applied to people who are already famous, and now become more famous. Focus on individuals suits the media as it sells papers and TV programmes. However, in different cultures, for example the Hindu culture, families and communities are more important than individuals. The culture itself is against egoism or self-promotion and publicity. The media cannot 'focus' on groups nor can it profit from them – it is much easier to glorify the individual. By its nature, culture is more subtle and complex and not easy to explain through media like television which have to make an immediate visual impact. Hence there are very few cultural icons or celebrities. As a result, there is a big loss here because the truth about an interdependent and mutual identity is not communicated. Thus we will not easily find many Indians living in the west who are celebrities, because they do not actively seek it.

Also the media today is often sensationalist and negative in many ways. It wants to focus on what will grab headlines and sell papers. It wants to promote gossip and give huge coverage to what celebrities are doing because this sells. The competition means that they are desperate for scoops and will send the paparazzi to hound and follow the celebrities. As there are no fixed quotas on the percentage of news devoted to covering diversity, nor is there any measure of the quality and sensitivity of diversity coverage, it is not easy to monitor actual performance.

Homogenisation

With the advent of global television there is a homogenising influence. Cultures of the west are sweeping the east and the values of materialism, sexual freedom, selfishness, alcohol and drugs are sweeping the planet. The more time people spend watching TV, the more their world becomes an illusion and they lose the contact with reality. Race and ethnicity gets submerged under this sweep and a lot of coverage is about the here and now and 'what's in it for me'. A 2007 survey by Weber Shandwick in the UK found that in advertising, companies often use ethnic minorities as token faces rather than in a culturally sensitive way. I sometimes look at a poster and think that the advertiser is really trying desperately to get a person who is black and white and brown at the same time to appeal to all audiences – I often wonder whether the picture is graphically manipulated to fit this!

The sense of history and heritage gets lost in the media process. People experience a temporary happiness accompanied by a long-term isolation and lack of identity. In the rush to go somewhere and be someone, respect for people with disability also gets lost as there is no patience. As to where we are going and what we are trying to achieve, and whether or not this will fulfil us, nobody knows. The media helps us to live in an illusory world.

There is also a huge commercial public relations industry which feed the media with 'news' and influences the way images and brands are portrayed – the crude word for this is 'spin'. The extent to which minority companies have PR skills will have an impact on the way they are understood and perceived. My experience of the UK is that there are very few organised ethnic minority media campaigns or organisations and most are private and commercially oriented.

Internet Power

The internet provides a free and open medium for ethnic minorities to express themselves and communicate without being restricted by a biased editor or newspaper. They can say what they like in a language and method that suits them. It is an amazing borderless technology whose shop is open 24/7. One does not need a passport to travel to the US or India via the internet and view its websites. This has led to an increase in the number of websites and blogs compiled by BME citizens. For example, Anup Shah, a young Jain, started his own website on global issues called www.globalissues.org which is very popular and visited by all kinds of people trying to understand the complex problems of modern living.

There is even an association for BME people working in the media which operates via a website, www.cultivasian.org. It tries to promote diverse events and debate and discussion on culture and the arts. I have several blogs of my own running, one of which is on 'Diversity' and the other on India in the twenty-first century entitled 'Century India'. My company Diverse Ethics Ltd (www.diverseethics.com) focuses on 'enabling respect through communication' and we publish a free monthly email Diverse Ethics Bulletin about diversity in Britain which is popular and growing.

The Media Trust is one of the largest media charities in the country, founded by the Channel 4 news broadcaster Jon Snow. It also has its own TV channel called the Community Channel which is broadcast free on digital. One of their excellent services is the community newswire, which enables small charities to circulate their news nationally through the Press Association. Details of the Media Trust and its services are at www.mediatrust.org.

Drama and Films

The biggest impact about perceptions comes about through mass media films such as popular serials like *EastEnders* and adapted dramas and novels. Here, rarely are script-writers from ethnic minority backgrounds. Richard Attenborough's award-winning film about Mahatma Gandhi was based on significant research and investment in authenticity and portrayal of the true life and achievements of this great soul. Attenborough managed to make it into a blockbuster movie through his skill, resources and influence. However, this is rare.

Gurinder Chadha has recently succeeded as an independent film director through films like *East is East, Bend It Like Beckham* and *Bride and Prejudice* which manage to be sensitive about Indian culture and clever and entertaining in their portrayal to a wide-ranging audience. Meera Syal has also made a huge contribution to comedy and film through her acting and novels. *Goodness Gracious Me* was a comedy series which was hailed as a huge breakthrough in cross-cultural communication through humour in this country, and the jokes were written and performed by Indians who, somehow, also managed to have editorial influence. There is a very famous sketch in this series where 'white' actors and producers make a proposal for a series to a BBC Board of Editors which is entirely coloured, and who ask very critical questions about the project and eventually reject it. This was a reverse pun. The point was well made – there is a lack of sensitivity to diversity in the media.

Disability is also rarely shown in the media, especially in prominent or popular programmes, although here again, things are improving fast. Recent exceptions have been in the children's programme *Tracey Beaker* in which the main character is a disabled girl (suffering from cerebral palsy), called Layla. On the BBC News, there is a security correspondent who appears often in a wheelchair (Frank Gardener). He was shot and paralysed whilst filming on duty in the Middle East, but has since continued to work for the BBC, who have accommodated his disability and given him a prime role. Generally speaking, few disabled people are given significant training and responsibility to rise to senior roles. This requires investment and a pro-active approach to enable all kinds of people to grow and flourish. If done well and sensitively, the public would be able to perceive disabled people as normal with the ability to excel just like everyone else. This is especially important to convey to those people who do not have any experience of physical disability in their families and do not understand that they are looking for acceptance, love and respect just like everyone else and not expecting special treatment. When done subtly through a story or a film, the impact is significant. It tells the audience that 'disabled' people are 'normal' and should be treated as such.

A Picture Speaks a Thousand Words

Photographs in newspapers and magazines also have a big impact on perception. If photos of black people generally only appear when they are arrested then this can convey the impression that they are usually criminals. Recently, I have noticed that reports do not readily specify the colour of the alleged criminals. Positive photographs have the opposite impact – they convey a culture in all its glory. Most people who have attended Hindu weddings know how colourful and vivid they are with all the sarees and the lovely food and large numbers of guests. Unfortunately, this rarely hits the news as it is not a news story, but it has now begun to appear in films and documentaries, so that those who have not been to these events can see the colour and gaiety of 'arranged' marriages! Also, there is no alcohol at these events and everyone who attends have a fabulous time and get along well with one another without any intoxicants.

The angle of a story is critical to its appearance in the media. Marriage is not normally news, but if it is a celebrity marriage, then it is news everywhere. The Stephen Lawrence murder continued to dominate the media because of the dogged persistence of his parents and their cooperation with the media. The angle here was injustice and racism to a young black teenager who had done nothing wrong. It is likely that this constant media coverage influenced the full government enquiry into the incident, leading finally to a major change in legislation which is having far reaching effects even today. What is a good story for *The Sun* may not be a good one for *The Guardian* as each paper has a different audience and editorial focus. *The Guardian* is regarded as a left of centre paper and often publishes unique features about what is happening to poor or underprivileged people or those who do not normally have public representation. It is a paper which represents the voice of the underdog. This cannot be said of *The*

Times or *The Financial Times*. Both *The Daily Mail* and *The Sun* seem to enjoy publishing scare-mongering stories about the rise of immigrants in this country. Rarely do they portray the strength and beauty of diversity.

Religion

Coverage of religion is poor and generally negative. The broadsheets give very few column inches to features on faith and usually there is one column in a little corner at the back once every week. Religious correspondents do not have much clout in the paper and the perception is that most religions are irrational, dogmatic and unscientific and do not have any space in a liberal enlightened society. Thus religious diversity and the huge range of festivals and worship which is peacefully and artistically conducted by religious communities gets barely any mention or coverage – except where there is a riot or conflict. The publication of the cartoons of Prophet Mohammed or the Pope's controversial speech about Islam became world-wide news within a matter of hours. The media thrives on controversy, and sometimes is moved to create it where none exists.

The local papers are keen to reach out to the community and different readers in the population. As a result, more positive news can be found about local groups and com-munity events with a desire to support and encourage them. They know that these stories will never reach the national press and actually do result in improved sales and readership. For example, *The East Anglian Daily Times* did a series on faith in Suffolk and BBC Suffolk likewise produced a series on different faiths. In my small town of Colchester, there are people from 91 countries living here, and I have proposed to the *Colchester Gazette* a series entitled 'A World in Colchester' to expose this diversity and show to Colchester its living strength. The editor liked the idea very much. Many of these papers are growing at the expense of the national papers because of this positivity and connectivity with their audiences. National papers can readily become distant from their readers if they are not too careful.

Bias

So as listeners or viewers, how do we avoid developing biased views of other cultures or peoples? How do we filter the stereotypical images from the genuine and positive depictions of culture, belief and equality which are conveyed in some broadcasts and articles? We clearly have a choice in what we watch and listen. We may develop a trust with some programmes and presenters over time e.g. David Attenborough's various series on nature, which we find educational and unbiased. We should also be conscious about the time we spend consuming the media as compared to social interaction, talking to colleagues or belonging to diverse social groups or organisations. Awareness of the editorial and filtering processes of the media will help us to watch out for biased programming and avoid it. Unfortunately, the bias is often subtle and sophisticated and we may not be able to notice it, but it can have a pervasive effect.

One practical way of eliminating bias is to give any new or different person we meet the benefit of the doubt. Pro-actively. All too often, people are suspicious of difference and their views get influenced by the stereotype images. For example, an Indian could be judged as someone who comes from a poor country (although this image is changing now as India become prosperous). A similar perception can exist of black Africans. In many cases, if you dig deeper, you may find that they can speak four languages, have a smile which stretches from ear to ear and have a keen sense of personal hygiene and dress. Often, they are self-taught in music, arts and, sometimes also, the English language. Rarely do they need our help but simply our respect and dignity. As humans, they too have a right to live and work. When they move into our neighbourhood, it could be an opportunity for diversity. But some people don't like 'which country do you come from?' as an opening question (though I personally do not mind). It can also be true that they were born and bred in Britain even though they have a different skin colour.

On 8 December 2006, the news was dominated by a speech by Prime Minister Tony Blair explaining that immigrants should integrate or get out. This was given prime coverage in all the radio and news channels and the BBC message board was inundated with a large number of comments about this speech. So even where there is a discussion about the whole matter of diversity itself, the media plays a key role in shaping it. The newspapers and media told us that this speech was well received by the general public, which is getting tired of all this multiculturalism. Again, the media interpreted this news for us, although they did not carry out any systematic survey of how people have reacted to the speech. On Channel 4 news, Mr Tariq Ali commented that it is unclear what British values are and it was also unfair for Tony Blair to target all immigrants as a result of terrorist acts of a select few. For some time, there has been a national debate about shared values, citizenship and multiculturalism. Many believe that Britain has gone too far to encourage difference and pander to the minorities rather than to ensure that cultures respect the laws and traditions of Britain. This debate will continue, but Britain should not forget that a large majority of the immigrants in this country are law abiding and respectful of others.

Whatever our personal views, the media have a major role in influencing them and shaping our understanding and judgements about others. It is not enough to say that if we don't like a newspaper or a TV programme, we can avoid buying it or switch it off. A free press is vital to a democratic country, and in the UK, there is a concentration of media ownership which is disturbing. Also, very few ethnic minorities or disabled people occupy senior positions at the editorial level in the media. Changes are afoot and there is a greater awareness of the legislative responsibility of diversity and some media are also seeing diversity as a commercial advantage. Time will tell about the difference this will make to our images and perceptions of others. There is a definite move to embrace diversity and a much greater awareness of the issues.

CHAPTER SUMMARY

- Media plays a major influence on our perceptions of others.

- Hitherto, the media had been mainly white, but there is a change going through the industry, with the BBC at the forefront.

- Editors have a major influence in filtering news and programmes and if they are biased, that would affect the programme.

- Ethnic minorities are now appearing on programmes as presenters and as journalists, although there are very few in senior editorial positions.

- Celebrities do dominate a big chunk of media today.

- The Media Trust is an excellent media charity which trains and supports community groups.

- Generally, it has little time to be authentic in the way it represents ancient cultures, although it is trying to learn.

- Black history and documentaries are few and far between.

- Advertising influences perceptions in very powerful and subtle ways.

- The internet is a large free and open space where there is huge diversity.

POINTS TO PONDER

- Be conscious of the limitations of media and potential for bias.

- When you see a programme you do not like, you can express your concerns via the internet. Also you can set up your own website or blog if you wish.

- Some media are biased against diversity and if you subscribe to them, you are subscribing to this world-view.

- Understand the strengths and limitations of each medium – radio, TV and print and make your choices accordingly.

- The internet has revolutionised media and also given much more power to individuals to influence and create their own media.

- The greater interactivity of media today gives you some influence on the broadcasts – you can call in and make comments.

- Campaign to have diverse editors and programme makers in powerful organisations.

- You can avoid the media by meeting people and listening to their experiences and stories directly – there is then no potential for bias as there is no medium!

Our Common Future

Britain has a lot going for it: a history of democracy, a liberal media, a cosmopolitan population, and a language which is being increasingly used throughout the world. There is a culture of respect and tolerance which is the envy of many countries of the world. The BBC is a national institution producing quality broadcasting and innovating constantly. Our education systems and institutions also attract thousands of students from all over the world who want to advance their understanding and knowledge. Embracing diversity in our minds, attitudes and actions is a huge positive step which in time can make us the global capital of culture, arts, learning and hospitality. But we are not there yet.

Diversity as Opportunity

One of the key reasons for this is that we still do not see diversity as an opportunity and not a threat. In a world which is increasingly global it helps to have the world at home. Monoculturalism creates sameness and conservatism whereas multicultural societies are open, tolerant and diverse in a positive way. The world is literally at home for us. Migrants are often hungry for work and opportunity and bring an enthusiasm and determination which uplifts a lot of people in different ways. They are resourceful and adaptable and bring their colours and spices with them to make our whole country colourful. Yes, it is important that everyone abides by the law, and one should remember that law-breaking is not just done by ethnic minorities and even white people break the law. Differences may cause some tensions, but these need to be addressed through engagement and dialogue rather than barriers and offensiveness.

Another of our drawbacks is our pride. Whilst it is good to be proud, it is not good to be arrogant or complacent. We need to understand our pride before we can be justly proud, and also understand the pride of others. Our innocence and curiosity should continue beyond our childhood into our adult life. By respecting others, we need not lose our own pride. If anything, we would grow in our sense of the world and our place in it. The difference that we have with others may cause tension and conflict, but it is in the way we address it and resolve it that will help nurture our common future.

Violence and terrorism have been an experience of human history for generations. People fight and religion may be a part of it, but it rarely is the whole story. Whilst all violence is abhorrent, we must start by making peace with ourselves and staying calm within so that we can have lasting freedom. The concerns of diversity have a link with issues like poverty, social exclusion, drugs and alcoholism and public health and morality. Although discrimination may emerge on the surface, its root causes may be much more complex than what people believe.

For example, if people live in ghettos and in poor working-class areas and discover that a certain ethnic group is doing better than the whites, it may lead to discrimination and even violence. It is the difference, and the relative success of one group which sticks out. The fact that most of the people are living very difficult deprived lives makes the threshold of tolerance very low and the levels of anxiety very high. As a society, it is our responsibility to address these economic inequalities, and even deal with the softer side of moral upliftment and family values alongside the educational and economic challenges. Mahatma Gandhi used to say, 'The religion of the poor is food – only when the stomach is full will they be able to reflect on life.' In other words, it is no use teaching morality to poor people if they have no food. We need to address the economic priorities first.

Elitism

Another of Britain's weaknesses is elitism. There is a focus on excellence in everything and vast resources and skills are devoted to it. The average or the middle gets forgotten. For example, the quality of our vocational training is very poor nationally. Similarly, the quality of our efforts in terms of economic regeneration is also variable and so are the outcomes. While there is good provision for adult education, employers rarely encourage or support ongoing training. The rate at which the world is changing today means that continuing education is vital to the future of our economy and country. The professional classes are also guilty of greed – especially if we look at many accountants, lawyers, doctors, dentists or pharmacists. Teachers are a rare exception. Rarely do professionals play a direct role in the improvement of the health of the nation or in helping improve social life or create vibrant communities. They are businesses first and professionals a poor second (and unequally rich financially!). Instead of ethics and standards being at the core of their services, they often become peripheral to commercial goals.

Whilst the law is helpful in protecting diversity, it should not promote fear and conservatism and people should see the positive opportunities that are presented. My concern is that organisations would restrict the number of ethnic minorities or disabled people entering the system in order to avoid any potential racial or disability concerns in future. In fact, I see this happening in practice and it is as if there is an attempt to sweep the problems under the carpet. This is the opposite of the intentions of the law which are to promote diversity and remove discrimination. I see the same thing happening in the area of age discrimination. Companies just do not employ older people for fear of any future problems they may have with them. In practice, it is very difficult to prove discrimination at the stage of recruitment by isolated and disempowered individuals.

In the area of employment and prospects for women, there has been significant progress made in recent years with a huge increase in employed women. In fact, one study has shown that women comprise 60 per cent of the workforce in Britain today. In terms of seniority, there is still work to be done and also pay rates are unequal in some circumstances. But progress is being made and organisations are becoming more and more aware of their duties and responsibilities. Childcare facilities and access to childcare has also improved, helping more women to remain in the workforce and pursue their careers.

Slow but Sure

Embracing cultural diversity is necessarily a slow process, and whilst it is important to highlight diversity and kick-start the change in the composition of the workforce, paradoxically, it is also important not to give too much public attention to it. Somehow, the diversity should become a natural part of operation and not something that we should need to shout out loud about. It should be subtle and pervasive rather than loud and abrasive. In this way, harmony becomes a natural component and it comes through with the results and achievements of the organisation. In a survey of the legal profession, some ethnic minority lawyers were very critical of the lack of diversity and the institutional racism which they perceived. However, none of them wanted special preferences in terms of promotion and opportunity as they felt these would also be counter-productive. Others would think they got there because of their colour rather than their skills or abilities.

Education is key to changing attitudes and beliefs. Educators therefore carry a huge burden of responsibility in promoting diversity and shaping the character of their students. The provision of free and quality public education throughout the country means that there is a huge opportunity for taking positive public action to bring about this change. I know from experience that schools are expected to promote diversity and have programmes and events which embrace it – otherwise, their inspectors will highlight weaknesses and require changes.

Responsible Media

In a similar vein, the media plays a hugely influential role in shaping our knowledge and perceptions. Responsible media will have a positive impact on the ways in which we embrace and live with diversity. Irresponsible media will unfortunately have the exact opposite impact because it can create greater suspicion of others, barriers to integration and sometimes even the perception that difference is a liability. Fortunately, the presence in this country of a large publicly accountable media in the shape of the BBC helps us keep diversity in check, and in recent years the BBC has taken huge strides to embrace diversity. Actors and presenters come from a variety of ethnic backgrounds. Older people, disabled people and even obese people are appearing on prime-time programmes. This goes against the industry norm of portraying young, slim and beautiful or famous people all the time. Commercial media, which is also a very large industry in this country, is beginning to embrace diversity as it sees a commercial opportunity of reaching diverse audiences and groups. However, by definition, their commitment to moral values is usually thin and they are often dictated by the advertisers in their content and output.

Faith is an emotive issue, and whilst it creates barriers, it also has a big effect on our morality and integrity as a nation, with many people of faith having a commitment to charity, community and devotion which is governed by their conscience. There can be tension between faith groups, although there is a large interfaith network in this country and many grassroots interfaith initiatives which try to encourage dialogue between different faith groups. What is key here is that the concept of pluralism be accepted by all faith groups and the leaders publicly acknowledge that there are different ways of seeing and knowing God and all must respect other religions and people of faith. Unfortunately, as Britain is predominantly a Christian nation, and as there has not been any significant public declaration against the mainstream view that there is only one God, there is an intolerance among the Christian leadership. Hindus and Jains who come from strong pluralist traditions find this view very difficult to understand and intolerant.

Secular Britons who are against faith of any kind should understand that all humans are driven by faith of some kind, whether it be in the material world or a spiritual world, and are worthy of respect and dignity as human beings. The quality press in this country is generally secular and there is an atmosphere of disdain for faith and followers of different religions. In my opinion, this is because of illiteracy and ignorance rather than a view developed through careful scientific study and analysis. It is true that no faith groups are perfect, but neither are secular groups perfect. For many cultures, everyday life and faith are deeply intertwined and cannot be separated easily from one another.

Empowerment and not Commands

Hierarchical and autocratic organisations necessarily have problems with embracing diversity and difference. And traditional British management and power structures operate along these lines. The white male leader is still the dominant model, and there is often significant power and status attached to such leaders. However, in the fast changing modern world of technological innovation and progress, such organisations are struggling to cope. There is a need to empower people across the organisation and to be open and respond speedily to change rather than wait for a direction from the top. Such organisational cultures are also much more open to diversity and power-sharing. Often, they will see it as an opportunity rather than a threat and embrace it positively and pro-actively.

There are very simple ways by which organisations can communicate their commitment to diversity. An annual multi-faith or international event for all staff can sometimes expose the diversity and strength of a large organisation which it may not even know it has. It will also give a positive signal to ethnic minorities that they are welcome and the employer supports their cultural identity. Having their websites and communication brochures reflect the diverse workforce are also powerful signals to job applicants about the actual commitment to diversity. Giving holidays or leave to staff for celebrating their annual festivals also shows respect for their religious beliefs and this can be even-handed for all staff so that no one feels left out.

Creativity

Somehow, organisations need to creatively and imaginatively convey to their employees that they do not need to make radical changes to their identities to fit in and assimilate. People are hired because of their skills and competencies, but that does not mean that they have to leave their culture behind when they turn up for work. Unfortunately, many employees feel that this is the reality and are forced to have separate identities which cause stress and therefore have an impact on productivity. Mentoring schemes, especially for minorities would help and support them in their career progression and ensure that there are different people at all levels of the organisation.

Food is another great way to communicate the strength and beauty of diversity. When a company serves multi-faith food at a party, it shows its sensitivity to other cultures and customs, and as everyone enjoys varied food (even those who are suspicious of diversity) it can be a subtle way of reinforcing the importance and strength of diversity within the organisation. I have often found that the food leads to dialogue about cultures and beliefs and therefore engagement about belief rather than denial.

Respect

In the fast-paced world we live in, there is little time for people to understand the complexity of different cultures and customs. There is also the pressure to perform and meet commercial targets and personal ambitions. Hence it can be easy to ignore or discriminate in such circumstances. Somehow, organisations and educators need to make efforts to convey this complexity to staff and students so that at the very least, they respect what they do not understand. Often, there is staggering ignorance and at the same time an ignorance about their ignorance. People often do not know what they don't know and this is a real problem.

Travel is a major source of education about diversity. It has increased significantly in recent years and so has the growth in the study of languages. As there is greater awareness about the world, people are more likely to adventure to foreign lands and learn about different cultures first hand by experiencing them directly. It opens up new possibilities and as managers and executives of companies often have to travel for business, some time could be allocated to enable them to understand the different cultures they trade with during these trips. This could broaden horizons significantly and also enhance commercial success. At root, companies and employees who trade internationally need to recognise that understanding and sensitivity to foreign cultures will help them trade more effectively in the long run. All businesses are not the same and do not operate in the same way across national boundaries.

Being born in a country which has a global language as its vernacular has its strengths and weaknesses. The strength is that it allows us immediately to connect to the global world. The weakness is that we become complacent and do not put any effort in learning other languages which are windows to other cultures. Hence we shut our eyes to the world without realising it. When I talk to young white people, I discover often that their travel aspirations are toward America or Australia. It appears that they prefer familiar territory both in terms of language and culture. Here they would not learn any foreign culture in depth nor need to learn any foreign language. Instead, if they are encouraged to travel to varying destinations or take a gap year out (for example) in Uganda, as the Channel 4 News anchor Jon Snow did to life-transforming effect, they will learn and progress significantly in their appreciation of diverse cultures.

Under the Skin

Ideally, a diverse mind should enable us to go 'under the skin' of others and understand their values and beliefs. This is physically impossible as we all know, but it is possible through the use of imagination. Therefore, art plays a hugely influential role in our perception of others – whether it is music, theatre and film, visual arts or literature. Here again, education through the arts can open up young minds to different cultures and enable them to appreciate the richness of diversity. Music perhaps has made the most progress here as it has fused various sounds from all over the world and in this way connected listeners to different rhythms and sounds of different cultures. I recently took a music CD of prayers from the Jain culture to a local school where my son studies and found that they loved it so much that they wanted to play it again in future. Even though the words were in Sanskrit, somehow the combination of the music and the chants were so soothing that language did not matter and the sounds carried with them this ancient culture of peace. I was surprised by the impact and suddenly realised how we have underplayed the potential of promoting Jain culture through art and music. Art opens up the curiosity and where this leads depends upon the viewer or listener. We must open up these windows and make them accessible to all souls.

Open-mindedness is a quality which cannot be taken for granted and needs to be cultivated and nurtured regularly. This is easy to begin with when we are babies, but slowly it gets tainted by our upbringing, environment and experiences. Also our personal values impact our mindset. The more selfish and self-centred we become, the less time we have for others in our lives, minds and hearts. Here it does not even matter whether or not they are from our own culture or belief because we are focused purely on ourselves. This creates barriers and does not help our open-mindedness. Our values close our minds and this becomes a sad predicament.

Innocence and Curiosity

Even where we think we have open minds, we should have an active sense of innocence and curiosity about others. When we meet strangers, we should start with a position of trust rather than one of suspicion. Only when we trust others will we allow them to trust us. And often we have very little to lose by trusting others and giving them the benefit of the doubt. At the very least, our mind will be exercised and we will learn something new. Just as we shower our bodies daily, we should learn also to shower our minds regularly.

Dialogue and engagement with people from all walks of life will help us to understand them better and develop greater respect. We should not shy away from it and make positive and pro-active efforts to talk to our neighbours and work colleagues. Humour can sometimes break barriers more effectively than anything else and we should try to use it to build bridges and connect with one another. Some people may be reserved by culture or habit. They do not mean harm, but dialogue is not in their nature. Here, we have to find different ways of getting them to talk and engage and also all of us need to try to be open and accessible in this world. The way things are developing, it is only those people who are open and willing to be transparent and accountable that will succeed in the long run. Secrecy and back-biting will inhibit our own progress and growth.

Good Communities

Neighbourhoods and communities are the microcosm of our lives. A healthy person leads to a healthy family, which inspires a healthy community. We cannot create health or peace in isolation. And once we start peering into our neighbourhoods and removing our semi-detached existence, we will discover the world at our doorstep. Many windows to foreign lands are lying in the extensions of our own homes. So for planning a trip to India, we need look no further for guidance then our Indian neighbour. In fact, it is possible that he or she will give you a pilot tour in your own neighbourhood by inviting you to a festival or celebration of some kind. Then there will be foods to try, colours to savour, and before you know it, your journey has already begun . . . An annual Diversity Day celebrated in towns and cities throughout

Britain would be a wonderful way of keeping the positive message alive in people's minds and allowing everyone to feel welcome and respected.

There is no hope in this world if we want our existence to be exclusive. It breaks the fundamental law of the universe which is interdependence – we are a product of the world and should not see ourselves in isolation from it. Even where we are white and 'normal' one day, it is possible that we could become disabled and 'abnormal' the next as a result of an accident and experience in our own life the evil of discrimination. However, we need not wait to experience it – we can avoid it simply through our understanding and enlightenment. There is enough room in this world for all to co-exist in peace and harmony. When we experience threat, we should seek to enlarge our mind rather than withdraw in fear and act in spite. As Mahatma Gandhi once tellingly said to a racist tormentor, 'You will find there is room for us all.'

CHAPTER SUMMARY

- Britain should see its huge diversity as an opportunity rather than a threat. Many windows to foreign lands are lying in the extension of our own homes.

- All the world's major cultures and languages have a home here, including many minor ones.

- British values of respect, politeness and diplomacy are invaluable in nurturing diversity.

- Obsession with power and control will lead to disempowerment and fear. Organisations should learn to empower their members.

- Faith builds communities of spirit and is a major force for moral values in British society.

- There is much more in common between us than is different, but that does not mean that we should ignore the differences or expect others to change their identities.

- Ego, arrogance and elitism will obstruct genuine respect for people from all walks of life, rich or poor.

- Hospitality is an age-old method of caring for the welfare of others without fear or prejudice. It can be applied universally.

- Ancient cultures are complex by their very nature, but we should try to understand them and accept our ignorance when we do not understand them.

- Imposing our beliefs and values on others is wrong for any society.

- The legal system and policing should be fair to all.

- The media can play a major role in building bridges of understanding and respect. It should exercise its influence responsibly.

- Open-mindedness is a quality which needs to be nurtured and replenished regularly. It requires patience and a curious and innocent approach to others.

- We should always be prepared to engage in dialogue with others, irrespective of their culture or beliefs.

- Communities are built by people and we should be willing to sacrifice our time and skills to create lasting communities.

- Art and creativity are unique bridges of diversity. It helps us to go under the skin of others.

POINTS TO PONDER

- We can make a difference in the world and there are often simple practical ways of doing so which can be very effective.
- We should see difference as an opportunity to learn and grow.
- Smiling or encouraging others does not cost a penny and helps build a much better quality of life and society.
- Dialogue and engagement will help us to understand one another better.
- Britain is an island, but the sea connects us to the whole world.
- We should be cautious of always sticking to the familiar.
- When we encounter stumbling blocks or resistance, we should look for creative solutions around it.
- In asking the neighbour or a stranger for advice or guidance, we are not infringing on their privacy.
- There is no border between human diversity and bio-diversity. We are all a part of the planet and universe.

Diversity Resources

LAW AND EMPLOYMENT RIGHTS

www.direct.gov.uk

This is a huge website about all aspects of government. It has an excellent resource on employee rights relating to discrimination in the employment section. A priceless resource if you suffer from discrimination and want to know your rights.

www.cre.gov.uk

Excellent website of the Commission for Racial Equality with information about rights and responsibilities, the law and research studies.

www.cehr.org.uk

This will be the new merged website of Commission for Racial Equality, Equal Opportunities Commission and Disability Rights Commission.

www.drc-gb.org

Website of the Disability Rights Commission.

www.acas.org.uk

Excellent advice on Diversity and Equality for Employers and ways of resolving disputes and conflicts. Also, the Advisory, Conciliation and Arbitration Service (ACAS) gives free and independent professional advice on all employment rights issues, and they have a telephone helpline on 0845 747 4747.

RESEARCH STUDIES

www.homeoffice.gov.uk/equality-diversity/race-relations/
Government's Strategy to Improve Race Equality and
Community Cohesion.

www.cre.gov.uk/research
This contains all research commissioned by the Commission for Racial Equality.

www.cipd.co.uk
Diversity in Business, How much progress have businesses made? 2006.

www.man.ac.uk
University of Manchester, Black Entrepreneurs Survey, 2006.

www.cre.gov.uk
Careers in Print Media – What people from ethnic minorities think, Mori Research/CRE, 2005.
Why Ethnic Minority workers leave London's Print Journalism sector, CRE, 2005.
The Decline of Britishness, 2006, Ethnos Research and Consultancy.
Citizenship and Belonging – What is Britishness? CRE/Ethnos Research, 2005.
Diversity in the Public Appointments Process in Scotland, Scottish Executive Social Research, 2003.

www.communities.gov.uk
Review of the Evidence Based on Faith Communities, Office of the Deputy Prime Minister, 2006

The Unequal Academy, Association of University Teachers, 2005.

Faith Communities Toolkit – CEL/Faith Regen. An excellent toolkit about faith which is available as a free download at www.centreforexcellence.org.uk.

Judicial Diversity – Findings of Consultation with Barristers, Solicitors and Judges, Department for Constitutional Affairs/Opinion Leader Research, 2006.

The Changing Face of Britain – Ethnic Minorities in the UK, Pocket Handbook, 2004.

Business in the Community/Lloyds TSB.

The Business Case for Diversity – Good Practices in the Workplace, European Commission/Focus Consulting, 2005.

Changing Faces – How we adopt our identity at work, Vodafone UK, 2006.

Sex and Power – Who Runs Britain? Equal Opportunities Commission, 2004. (www.eoc.org.uk)

'The British and how to deal with them', Ram Gidoomal, Deepak Mahtani and David Porter, Middlesex University Press, UK, 2001.

MEDIA

For a full listing of ethnic and diverse media, go to Guardian Media Guide *or an alternative listing of media organisations such as* Willings Press Guide.

www.mediatrust.org

> An excellent organisation providing training and support to charities and community organisations about media.

www.globaltolerance.com

www.catalystmagazine.org

> Website of the magazine on equality and diversity published by the Commission for Racial Equality. You can subscribe to this quality magazine for free by registering on the website.

www.guardian.co.uk

> *The Guardian* website is an excellent resource for news and features relating to diversity. The search engine is

excellent and so is the quality of the articles and writing – and it is all accessible for free!

COMMUNITY DEVELOPMENT AND LOCAL GOVERNMENT

www.idea-knowledge.gov.uk

This is an excellent site for local government initiatives on equality and diversity, including ideas and resources.

www.cdf.org.uk

The site of the Community Development Foundation, a non-profit organisation which champions Community Cohesion and gives grants to faith and community organisations.

www.communities.gov.uk

This is the website of the Department for Communities and Local Government with excellent resources and information on equality and diversity. This includes the strategy report: 'Improving Opportunity, Strengthening Society'.

ARTS AND DIVERSITY

www.artscouncil.org.uk

This is the main website of the Arts Council, the national body for funding and promotion of the arts. Equality and diversity is a major part of its remit, and it is seriously committed to it. Creativity and the arts are one of the best ways of building bridges between cultures and peoples.

EDUCATION AND COURSES

www.bl.uk

The British Library in London is the best national resource for information in the UK.

www.vam.ac.uk
>   Website of the Victoria and Albert Museum and a very good resource for cultural information and events.

www.nationalschool.gov.uk
>   National School of Government – the centre for education of senior civil servants in the UK.

www.busman.qmul.ac.uk
>   Queen Mary College of the University of London has a Centre for Research on Equality and Diversity at the Business School.

www.soas.ac.uk
>   The School of Oriental and African Studies, London University. This also has an excellent Centre for Jaina Studies.

www.festivalshop.co.uk
>   Produces a good catalogue of educational resources for diversity.

CONSULTANTS

www.focusconsultancy.co.uk
>   Focus Consultancy does surveys and research, training and education in the area of equality and diversity.

www.diverseethics.com
>   Diverse Ethics Ltd is a specialist in diversity strategy, training and research.

FUNDING RESOURCES

www.cdf.org.uk
>   The Faith Communities Capacity Building Fund gives grants to faith-based organisations in Britain. It is managed by the Community Development Foundation.

www.lotteryfunding.org.uk
The National Lottery also awards grants for specific community development or heritage projects by non-profit organisations.

EMPLOYMENT

www.publicappointments.org.uk
A great site for all kinds of senior public jobs – paid and unpaid – to join advisory boards on regional and national bodies. They are really emphasising applications from diverse range of people.

www.civilservice.gov.uk/diversity
The site of the major national campaign (10 point plan) to ensure the Civil Service has a diverse staff base.

NETWORKS

www.interfaith.org.uk
Site of the UK interfaith network

www.niace.org.uk/bpln
Black Practitioners and Learners Network

www.nationalbpa.com
National Black Police Association

www.sifre.org.uk
Website for Suffolk Inter-faith Resources

DIVERSE SPACES

www.stethelburgas.org
A multi-faith centre for reconciliation and peace in Central London

www.mandir.org
The beautiful Swaminarayan Hindu Temple in London

www.oshwal.org
   The site of the new Jain temple in Potters Bar, North
   London

www.jaincentre.net
   Site of Jain temple in Leicester

www.bkwsu.org
   The Brahmakumaris World Spiritual University

BOOKS

Bloody Foreigners – The Story of Immigration to Britain
   Robert Winder, Abacus, 2004

Immigrants – Your Country Needs Them
   Phillipe Legrain, Little Brown, 2007

The Jain Path – Ancient Wisdom for the West
   Aidan Rankin, 'O' Books, 2006

www.diverseethics.com

DIVERSE ETHICS LTD provides consultancy, training and support in all areas of Diversity and Corporate Social Responsibility. Our particular expertise is in media and communication. Contact us for:

- Unique staff training seminars and retreats
- Strategy and advice on benefiting from diversity
- Communications and Public Relations advice
- Advice and support relating to Indian culture and spirituality
- Public speaking and lectures on diversity

For more details and to subscribe to our complimentary monthly Diverse Ethics Email Bulletin, visit:
www.diverseethics.com

Contact Address:
Diverse Ethics Ltd, 9 Redmill, Colchester, CO3 4RT, UK
Dr Atul K. Shah, Chief Executive
Tel: 07804 294903
Email: atul@diverseethics.com